I0152166

"Dr. Lance Alexander is a powerful man of God who understands God's Word, His Will, and His Ways. He has a profound understanding of God's process for helping us walk closer with Him and to develop a stronger walk of faith. Dr. Alexander, a powerful prophet of God, effectively crystallizes seven essential rules that we need to understand in order to help us successfully walk through the many transitions of life. *Transition* has been written through the pen of maturity and experience by someone who walks in the supernatural favor of God. It is a word of encouragement. It is a word of wisdom and understanding. It is a word of instruction. It is a word of blessing. I encourage you to read this book, absorb the concepts, and apply them to your life. I know that you will be blessed as I was blessed."

—**Apostle Ric Steele**
Due Season Christian Church, Intl

"I absolutely *love* this book of guidance and answers! I stand in awe of Lance's ability to hear, interpret, and share godly solutions with those facing turbulent times. For many years now, Lance has been faithful to the study of God's Word and has used great wisdom as he also transitioned our family through the storms of life. As you read this book, I sincerely believe your mind will be renewed and opened to God's answers for any life-changing transition that you may experience. Get ready... Let the 'Transition' begin!

Lance, I'm so proud of you! The completion of this book was in your destiny all along. The selfless hours, days, and nights that you spent in preparation for this writing will cause others' dreams to come true as they find their way through the storm! You are beyond inspiring and your book is a brilliant piece of work!"

—Vernell Alexander

TRANSITION

HOW TO RESPOND
WHEN GOD
CHANGES YOUR PLANS

DR. LANCE ALEXANDER

HIGH BRIDGE BOOKS
HOUSTON

Transition: How to Respond when God Changes Your Plans
By Lance Alexander

Copyright © 2016 by Lance Alexander
All rights reserved.

Printed in the United States of America
ISBN (Paperback): 978-1-940024-75-2
ISBN (eBook): 978-1-940024-76-9

High Bridge Books titles may be purchased in bulk for educational, business, fundraising, or sales promotional use. For information please contact High Bridge Books via www.HighBridgeBooks.com/contact.

Scripture taken from the New King James Version®. Copyright © 1982 by Thomas Nelson. Used by permission. All rights reserved.

Published in Houston, Texas by High Bridge Books

CONTENTS

ACKNOWLEDGEMENTS

My deepest appreciation...

To Vernell. Thanks for being my wife, best friend, most-faithful supporter, co-laborer in the ministry, loving mother to our children, and lover. You are truly God's gift to me, and I value and treasure you. I love you, "Baby Girl."

To Rivers of Life Church International. All of you have brought great joy to our lives. You each are dear to my life. Thank you for sharing in the call of God and encouraging me in the ministry.

To Gulf Coast family Superintendent Grayling and Heronica Alexander Faith Temple, Evangelists Lynson and Patti Alexander Ministries, Pastor Darwin and District Missionary Jean Pouncy, Missionary Ellen Allison, Elder Gerry Howard, Elder Lloyd Alexander III, Professor Pandora Alexander, Evangelist Christopher Alexander, and last but not least... my father and mother, Lloyd and Mother Betty J. Alexander who gave us the richest inheritance of all time: Jesus Christ.

To our many ministerial friends and to name a few... Apostle Rick and Pastor Kathy Steele, Due Season Ministries; Dr. Walter and Pastor Tiny Latson, Fruit of the Spirit; Dr. Russell and Apostle Michelle Grigsby, Exousia Ministries; Dr. Kathy and Milton Hostetler, professional growth association; Apostles Earnest and Ora Jackson, missionaries to Ghana, Africa.

Especially to our Pastors, Dr. Rick V. and Dr. Barbara Layton of Refreshing Point Ministries in Shreveport Louisiana who have always been there for us with love and guidance over the past 15 years.

INTRODUCTION

How did this teaching come about? Hurricane Katrina, one of the greatest storms in the history of America, was about to hit the Gulf Coast region. My mother and 12 other relatives and friends were coming to live with my wife and me until they were able to return to their homes. They had waited too late to secure a place to live away from the coastline. I was the pastor of a ministry here in this city, and the people who knew me as a child were now going to be guests in our home. And yes, they would also attend services at our church for the next few weeks or more.

I left the family church denomination some years ago and was now pastor of a non-denominational, independent church that God told me to build. My mother and two sisters who were with her are evangelists. I knew at some point during their stay that I would be ministering to them. I wasn't sure they would want to hear anything I had to say because they saw me as "just" their brother.

After much prayer, I heard the Spirit of the Lord say, "I'm downloading to you what to say." By the Spirit, I heard the word, "transition." From this point forward, God began to impart the meaning of "transition" one piece at a time. This download of information came to me during each service we had while they were with us.

The first service was centered on understanding the definition of "transition." This was critical to understanding the rest of the messages. These next services would encompass instruction for everyone, spiritually and secularly.

I knew it was God's plan for them to make it through this transition period.

Transition is the moving of people and things from one place to another. Whenever you are going to move things or people from one place to another, you will need to have rules and plans for moving them that will ensure their safety and effectual arrival.

Here are the Seven Rules of Transition for those who were surviving the worst storm ever on the Gulf Coast.

CHAPTER 1

BEING LED BY HIS SPIRIT

By the Spirit, I received Rule One for moving people and things safely and effectually: You must be led by the Spirit!

At first, this seemed deep and religious to me. I sensed that the Lord was saying, "Remember, Son, I only deal with you according to your spirit and not your head. What you know will not be the leader in this disaster." I was led to this scripture to confirm what I had heard.

> The spirit of man is the candle of the Lord, searching all the inward parts of the belly.
> (Prov. 20:27)

God uses man's spirit to lead him around like a person uses a candle to see where he is going in the dark. When a storm like this hits you in the dark, most of the time, it's because you don't know what is going to happen next. Forecasters try to predict by using information they have as they go, but God wants to lead you by your spirit if you will allow Him to do so. Wow! Isn't God good? He wants to lead us to a safe place in Him.

> For as many as are led by the Spirit of God, they
> are the sons of God. (Rom. 8:14)

If we are led by the Spirit of God, we have now become the children of God. Our earthly fathers would not lead their families into peril or disasters and neither would God, our Heavenly Father. The key is being led by the Spirit of God.

People are sometimes led by a lot of things that are not designed to be leaders. Here are a few examples.

Led by money or paycheck...

Never let money lead you in taking a job because money is not what determines success.

Led by what you think...

Unless your mind has been renewed by the Word of God, it is full of pride and secular methods.

Emotions...

Emotions were designed by God and are good for us, but they were not designed to be our leaders.

The status of the 401K...

Earthly wealth is good, but heavenly wealth is better. And heavenly wealth is eternal.

Best friend who knows everything...

They have a best friend, who has a best friend, and there is no telling from what source he or she got that wisdom.

Past family traditions…

Everything our families have taught us is not always Bible based.

God just said He will lead us by His Spirit. It's not about how much money we have because, when God is leading, He will cause us to have what we need when we need it.

Don't be led by money. Money can answer a lot of things, but it is not always the answer. I have found that, in God, if we purpose in our hearts to do anything for the Kingdom's sake, money will come. First, purpose in your heart, and if it's done in faith, it will come to pass.

> Every man according as he purposeth in his heart, so let him give; not grudgingly, or of necessity: for God loveth a cheerful giver. And God is able to make all grace abound toward you; that ye, always having all sufficiency in all things, may abound to every good work: As it is written, He hath dispersed abroad; he hath given to the poor: his righteousness remaineth forever. (2 Cor. 9:7-9)

Years ago, my mother and father had to be evacuated. My father was still living and was on a life-support system. He needed urgent medical care. We did not know how to make this transition happen. They were not sure if we could reach them in time and were literally planning to stay in the storm and even die together if they could not get out together. We were not going to allow them to stay. Doors were opened by FEMA to evacuate him and my mom at no cost. Praise God! It's God's will for us to be led safely and effectually.

People are too often led by what they think rather than what the real truth of the matter is. The truth for believers is that God wants to lead us and that it is His good pleasure to give us the Kingdom.

> Having predestinated us unto the adoption of children by Jesus Christ to himself, according to the good pleasure of his will. (Eph. 1:5)

Another point we gave the people living with us and others who had evacuated was that we are not to be led by our emotions. We acknowledge the fact that God has designed us with emotions and that they are good. However, when we look at the purpose and design of our emotions, we find that they were never designed to lead us but to tell us something is going on with us. Emotions are *indicators*. They indicate a range of feelings we have so we can address what is going on.

If you are feeling an indication of heaviness or sadness, the response as a believer is to put on the garment of praise and not to keep feeling sad.

If you have the indication of sorrow from a loss of any kind, the Word of God tells us what the response to that indicator of loss should be. And that is to not feel sorrow as the world does who has no hope, but if and when we express sorrow, it should be with the knowledge that God will restore and that our loved ones are with Him.

> But I would not have you to be ignorant, brethren, concerning them which are asleep, that ye sorrow not, even as others which have no hope. (1 Thess. 4:13)

Anyone who is emotionally led will end up in disaster because emotions do not make good leaders. Why? Because they are without boundaries and instructions. Emotions have to be taught, trained, and dealt with according to the Word of God, or else they will be out of control and often irrational.

Let's be led by the Spirit of God because He is our Father, and we can call on him as Father.

> For every one that asketh receiveth; and he that seeketh findeth; and to him that knocketh it shall

be opened. If a son shall ask bread of any of you that is a father, will he give him a stone? or if he ask a fish, will he for a fish give him a serpent? Or if he shall ask an egg, will he offer him a scorpion? If ye then, being evil, know how to give good gifts unto your children: how much more shall your heavenly Father give the Holy Spirit to them that ask him? (Luke 11:10-13)

The Spirit itself beareth witness with our spirit, that we are the children of God: And if children, then heirs; heirs of God, and joint-heirs with Christ; if so be that we suffer with him, that we may be also glorified together. (Rom. 8:16-17)

The Father will never lead you wrong. The only way He will lead you is by your spirit and with His Word.

How will you know when your spirit is leading you or if another spirit is trying to lead you? You will know by the peace you have in following the Word of God. Peace always follows God's leading. No peace follows the spirit of the enemy. When there is no peace, you must stop and wait for peace to return. Do nothing! When there is no peace, it will show up in your emotions, indicating something is wrong. Don't go past your peace and don't override your peace for anything!

God is a Spirit: and they that worship him must worship him in spirit and in truth. (John 4:24)

God will never talk to your mind. We are to renew our minds because an un-renewed mind will not receive truth.

And be not conformed to this world: but be ye transformed by the renewing of your mind, that ye may prove what is that good, and acceptable, and perfect, will of God. (Rom. 12:2)

God does not speak to our human logic or reason. He said His ways are not our ways.

For as the heavens are higher than the earth, so are my ways higher than your ways, and my thoughts than your thoughts. For my thoughts are not your thoughts, neither are your ways my ways, saith the LORD. (Isa. 55:8-9)

BEING LED BY HIS SPIRIT

Well, Brother Lance, what is the Spirit? Simply put, the Word of God is His Spirit, and the Spirit is His Word.

And the Word was made flesh, and dwelt among us, (and we beheld his glory, the glory as of the only begotten of the Father,) full of grace and truth. (John 1:14)

In the beginning was the Word, and the Word was with God, and the Word was God. The same was in the beginning with God. All things were made by him; and without him was not anything made that was made. (John 1:1-3)

If we have the Word of God on whatever it is we are trying to do, we have His Spirit because His Spirit is His Word, and His Word is His Spirit.

Child of God, whatever you are trying to do, get God's Word on it first because the Word of God will never fail. The problem with most people is that they have a word, but it is not God's Word. When you have the wrong word, you get wrong results, or you will get ungodly results.

Some people have Big Momma's or Big Poppa's word on it...

The bank's word on it...

Best friend's word on it...

The job's word on it...

Some philosophy's word on it...

The problem with having another person's word on whatever you are doing is they have to stand behind that word and make it good. Some people give their word and stand so far behind it you can't find them when it's time to make that word good.

How can you get God's Word on it? Find out what His Word says about it, and do it! Don't do "close to it", but do exactly what It says and how It says to do it. This would involve reading, studying, and meditating on the Word of God. For example, if you want the Word of God on how to live a prosperous life, you should find everything in the Bible that deals with "living prosperous" and then do it. If you want to find out how to have friends, find out what the Bible says about having friends.

> A man that hath friends must shew himself
> friendly: and there is a friend that sticketh closer
> than a brother. (Prov. 18:24)

Get the Word of God on it! God is not spooky and mysterious like some people think He is. He has given to us His Word to lead us and guide us in all areas of life. Yes! We have Holy Spirit as our teacher who comes beside us to help us. But if we have no Word, we have no help.

Remember that the candle of the Lord is man's spirit and that God is a Spirit. So, when God's Spirit comes into our spirit after being born again, we have the Spirit of Truth in us at all times. When something comes to us that is not truth, it will cause your spirit to be troubled out of peace if we don't reject it. That is being led by the spirit.

THE WILL OF GOD IS HIS WORD

Know the will of God. Simply put, the will of God is the Word of God, and the Word of God is His will.

> Jesus answered and said unto him, If a man love me, he will keep my words: and my Father will love him, and we will come unto him, and make our abode with him. He that loveth me not keepeth not my sayings: and the word which ye hear is not mine, but the Father's which sent me. (John 14:23-24)

> But whoso keepeth his word, in him verily is the love of God perfected: hereby know we that we are in him. (1 John 2:5)

Get the Word of God, and you will have God's will. It's that simple.

However, it is simple, but it is not easy having the Word of God and being led by the Word of God.

It is simple to read the Word of God, but rightly dividing the Word of God is important to ensure you have not taken the Word of God out of context. Let the Word speak for itself by keeping it context, the Word interpreting the Word. Here are a few principles to bear in mind.

LET SCRIPTURE INTERPRET SCRIPTURE

We need to put Scriptures in context with other Scriptures and with the rest of the chapter. In John 12:31-32, Jesus was referring to the judgment on sin in the world and the drawing of all sin to Him. However, most people read this as meaning that Jesus being lifted up would cause people to come and be saved. The scripture plainly is saying all judgment will be placed on Jesus and not on the world in order for the world to receive salvation.

DO NOT READ ANYTHING INTO THE SCRIPTURE THAT IS NOT THERE

Read its true meaning. Romans 3:20-23 is one example. Analyzing verse 23 incorrectly makes it look like a condemning statement from the Old Covenant. Verse 20 tells us that the Law does not justify us in God's eyes. Verse 21 refers to the Covenant of Grace minus the Law. Verse 22 establishes that we need faith in Jesus to be made righteous; it says nothing about works.

READ THE MEANING OUT OF THE SCRIPTURE, NOT INTO IT

> Let your women keep silence in the churches: for
> it is not permitted unto them to speak; but they
> are commanded to be under obedience, as also
> saith the law. (1 Cor. 14:34)

This scripture has been brutalized by so many who have read into it that women are not ever to speak in the church. This was a correction being made by Paul in this particular church at this one time because things were getting out of order due to everyone trying to speak at once or all prophesying in the same assembly. Nowhere else in the Bible will you find the Word of God telling women they must be quiet in the church or that they have no voice in the church. Many churches would have to close down in America and across the world if this were the correct interpretation.

LET THE SCRIPTURE LEAD YOU

Let the Word of God shine the light in the direction you should go, and you will always reach the destination God has planned for you. Being led by the Spirit is not some spooky, religious, hidden thing or a method that is only for certain people to have access. Being led by the Spirit is taking God's Word and using it to be our guide.

> Thy word is a lamp unto my feet, and a light unto
> my path. (Psa. 119:105)

A LIGHT TO GUIDE YOU

I used to be very frightened about the notion of being led by a spirit. I didn't think it could be done until I understood the Word of God as being a leader and my spirit as the vehicle. It is not that deep once you receive the understanding of the Word being a lamp to guide you on the path of life. Look at this scripture:

> The spirit of man is the candle of the LORD,
> searching all the inward parts of the belly.
> (Prov. 20:27)

In other words, God will communicate with your spirit, and your spirit will then communicate the message by shining a light on the Word in you. Your spirit light will turn on just like turning on a light switch in a dark room, helping you to see where you are and where you need to go. God will only communicate with our spirit because He is a Spirit. He will never communicate with your head or directly to your mind or thinking.

> God is a Spirit: and they that worship him must worship him in spirit and in truth. (John 4:23)

Our spirit is complete and pure, and God speaks to us by the Spirit and not our intellect. Man's intellect or thinking can be wrong. The Spirit of God is never wrong, so a person who is born again of the Spirit also will not be wrong. Once regenerated, your spirit is complete, and it will then bear witness to the truth. In other words, your regenerated, complete spirit is like a truth detector. It knows when the truth is present and will not want to follow error.

We can force our spirit to accept something that is error, but we will not be at peace if we do. For example, once you are born again and you try to visit places you know are not honoring to God, your spirit will not be at peace, but you can override your spirit and go all the same. When your peace is gone, stop, and go no further! Remember to follow peace because that is the leading of God.

Once I understood what the Word of God said about being led by the Spirit of God, it was not spooky and difficult. At that point, my life began to change. My trust in God grew more and more. Sometimes, we make things harder than they are supposed to be.

> Wisdom is the principal thing; therefore get wisdom: and with all thy getting get understanding. (Prov. 4:7)

Wisdom is knowing what to do with the knowledge God has made available. God has made available for us to be led by His Spirit. Therefore, choose to be led.

Here is an example of knowing when your spirit is communicating with you. I am going to ask you a question. First, give the answer in an audible voice. Then, the second time, answer the question without being audible. Here is the question: Have you received the Lord Jesus as your personal Lord and Savior? Now, without being audible, answer the same question and ask yourself, "Where did the answer come from, and who did it sound like?" Most people say they think it came from their mind or head. Then, when I ask who it sounded like, 99 percent of the people would say, "Like me." It sounds like you because it is you. You are not talking to yourself, but your spirit man is talking. The real you is the spirit man.

Man is a tri-union being: spirit, soul, and body. The real you is a spirit man. God breathed into man the (spirit) breath of life, and then he became a living soul that lives in a body.

> And the LORD God formed man of the dust of the ground, and breathed into his nostrils the breath of life; and man became a living soul. (Gen. 2:7)

Your spirit voice sounds just like you because it is you. Have you ever said, "Something told me not to do that"? Who do you think that *something* is? It is your spirit warning you, prompting you. Have you noticed that your spirit always wants to do the right thing and will if he is allowed? That is right. Your spirit can be overridden by an un-renewed mind that does not know the Word of God or a body that is out of control and not brought under subjection to the principles and statues of the Word of God.

You have a spirit, and I recommend being led by the spirit and not by your mind or your body. Can you imagine being led by your body? Your body in the lead would eat ice cream and cake for breakfast and hamburgers every day. Your mind, if not renewed by the Word of God, would be a disaster because some of the most ungodly thoughts imaginable would have the opportunity to lead you. I choose to be led by the Spirit of God, which is the Word of God.

CHAPTER 2

KNOW WHO'S LEADING YOU

"For as many as are led by the Spirit of God, they are the sons of God."

—Romans 8:14

As I began ministering to my family members who had evacuated from the Gulf Coast, I had to be aware that these were family members who had seen me grow up as a child and had not seen me develop into the man of God standing before them during this time. I began by sharing illustrations of how people are often led by their natural senses, past traditions, or by the sayings of great and powerful "Oz" characters in their families. You know the story of the "Wizard of Oz" where the main characters were trying to get to see the wizard to find answers for all of their problems. Many families have "wizards of Oz" who give out answers that are not always according to Scripture or not always true. Their ideas have just been passed down from one generation to another, and no one has stopped to ask, "What's the source?" or "Why is it true?"

In order to be led, it's critical to know who is leading you. You may have a person who is being emotionally led and that is not a good place to be. People that are led by their emotions are subject to their feelings and will be easily put off track. Just because something feels good does not mean it *is* good. Emotions were never meant to be leaders.

All of our emotions are good and were given to us by God. However, emotions were never designed by God to lead us. Emotions are indicators that something is going on and should be addressed. When your fuel indicator in your car is reading low, it is indicating something needs to be done. You are approaching a point for refueling. The fuel indicator does not say what octane fuel should be used or how to get to the fuel. It only indicates the status to allow you time to do something about it.

When you feel pain, it is an indication something is happening and needs to be addressed, but it does not lead you to the problem or solution. When you are sad, your sadness is indicating something is wrong, but it does not tell you what to do to correct the problem. I have found that, when emotions are in the lead, you will make bad decisions because emotions do not consider truth, facts, or strategies to determine what should be done. Emotions use what you can see, touch, hear, smell, and taste. Vegetables do not all look good, but they are good for the body. You can't always go by what you see either because things change. Things that appear to be one way may not be that way at all.

> While we look not at the things which are seen, but at the things which are not seen: for the things which are seen are temporal; but the things which are not seen are eternal. (2 Cor. 4:18)

We cannot always go by what we see. There are times when I have spoken to a person, and the person did not respond as I anticipated. My mind said that their actions toward me were strange. But the truth was that their mind was on other issues at the time. The person was not even thinking about me or anyone else. The person was just trying to make it through another day.

Choose not to let emotions, bad news, traditions, or anything that is not of God to be your leader.

EMOTIONS ARE GOD GIVEN

Emotions are God given, but they must be developed and used according to their original intent. For example, anger is an emotion mostly considered to be negative and harmful. However, God did not design anger to be a negative or harmful emotion. In fact, anger can be used in many positive ways. It can stir people to great accomplishments. Here is another one of those scriptures where people have taken the text out of context.

> Be ye angry, and sin not: let not the sun go down
> upon your wrath. Neither give place to the devil.
> (Eph. 4:26-27)

The scripture is saying to be angry but not to sin. It is okay to be angry, but it is not okay to choose sin as a response to our anger. Put another way, we can respond to our anger without being negative. I choose to respond in meekness or love to the situation.

If I choose a negative way to release my anger, I will give the devil an open door to get involved in my situation.

Anger, as it has been portrayed so many times, is not a bad emotion, but anger improperly released is not good. God gave us emotions to help us navigate through life, but they are not designed to lead us in life.

In light of these principles, understand that you can choose godly responses to people and to the things going on as you transition through the major storm events of life.

> A soft answer turneth away wrath: but grievous
> words stir up anger. (Prov. 15:1)

The LORD is gracious, and full of compassion;
slow to anger, and of great mercy. (Psa. 145:8)

Let's conform to the Word of God. Let's choose to use soft answers that will turn away wrath and be slow to get angry because it may well help to avoid the wrong response to anger.

Here's a tip for avoiding wrong responses to difficult confrontations: Remember that it's the first few minutes of any conversation that will set the tone for the entire conversation.

WE HAVE TO GROW PAST OUR RAISINGS

Many families have their own ways and customs. However, if we are going to live with excellence in our lives, God intends for us to go past our raising. This is because many people have not been raised according to the Scripture but according to some family tradition. For example, I have heard it said in my family, "What happens in this house stays in this house!" I agreed to that as a child. However, I went past my raising because there were things happening in the house that were wrong. Had I been exposed to some higher authority, our growth and development would have been much better. The Word of God does not say to hide anything. In truth, it says that whatever you hide will someday come to the light. Because of family traditions, we have hidden things to our detriment.

Beware lest any man spoil you through philosophy and vain deceit, after the tradition of men, after the rudiments of the world, and not after Christ. We are followers after Christ. (Col. 2:8)

Forasmuch as ye know that ye were not redeemed with corruptible things, as silver and gold, from your vain conversation received by tradition from your fathers; But with the precious blood of Christ, as of a lamb without blemish and without spot. (1 Pet. 1:18-19)

There was a woman who cooked the best-tasting pot roast of all of the women in the family. She cooked it for every family homecoming. Everyone would just marvel at how delicious the pot roast was and talk about it endlessly.

After many years of hearing how good her pot roast was, a family member asked the woman what the secret was to cooking this pot roast that made it so tender and delicious. The woman began by saying it was handed down from several generations and went on to say the secret, as told to her, was to cut off the ends of the roast before cooking.

One year later, by chance, she had the opportunity to talk to the person who had originated the tasty pot roast story. She asked her, "If one wanted it to be so tender and delicious, why was it so important to cut off the pot roast ends before cooking?"

The originator of the legend said that the reason she cut off the corners of the roast had nothing to do with making the roast tender. She cut the corners off the roast because it was too big for the small pan in which she cooked it. So, for many years this story was handed down, instructing people to cut the corners off to make it tender. That recipe was wrong.

How many things have been handed down in your family that are just wrong? Why do we heed so many traditions without asking, "Why?"

This storm was being talked about like a pot roast. We won't leave "come hell or high water," they said. That's just how our family responds to such things. And people were preparing to stay because of traditions handed down without any one stopping and asking why it was done *that* way.

> For as many as are led by the Spirit of God, they
> are the sons of God. (Rom. 8:14)

Let's break this truth down.

First, only a few will be so led. In other words, not many will be so led. Certainly, not everyone.

Second, it says "by the Spirit of God." We know who is leading.

Third, it opens up another door of opportunity to the person who will be led by the Spirit. He or she can enjoy being a son or daughter of God. Sons and daughters have rights and privileges that servants do not have. Even in the natural, our children will be our children, good, bad, or indifferent. We are still their parents, and we love them no matter what.

Not many people will know how easy it is to be led by the Spirit of God.

> Enter ye in at the strait gate: for wide is the gate, and broad is the way, that leadeth to destruction, and many there be which go in there at. Because strait is the gate, and narrow is the way, which leadeth unto life, and few there be that find it. (Matt. 7:13-14)

To be led by the Spirit of God, you must first be born again and then be Spirit filled. That sounds complicated, but it is not.

Being born again simply means to ask Christ to be your Lord and Savior by thanking him for forgiving you of all your sins at Calvary and inviting Him into your heart. Second, after being born again, just receive the baptism of the Holy Spirit as the Scripture says:

He that believeth on me, as the scripture hath said, out of his belly shall flow rivers of living water. (John 7:38)

Jesus could not do any miracles until he was baptized in the Holy Spirit.

Now when all the people were baptized, it came to pass, that Jesus also being baptized, and praying, the heaven was opened, And the Holy Ghost descended in a bodily shape like a dove upon him, and a voice came from heaven, which said, Thou art my beloved Son; in thee I am well pleased. (Luke 3:21-22)

Even Jesus needed the Holy Spirit to function on earth. Jesus was on planet earth for 30 years before it says the Spirit descended on him like a dove. This meant that, until the anointing of the Spirit came on Him, there were no miracles or mighty works done.

Once this filling has taken place, the Spirit of God will lead you by that same Holy Spirit. He can lead you in several ways. I prefer the way of peace. Man is a spirit who possesses a soul and lives in a body. God is a Spirit, and they that worship Him and are led by Him must do so and be so by the Spirit—in other words, Spirit to spirit.

> The spirit of man is the candle of the Lord,
> searching all the inward parts of the belly.
> (Prov. 20:27)

God uses man's spirit as a candle to lead him. God speaks to man's spirit only. He never communicates with your head or your body but only your spirit. The Holy Spirit leads with peace. When you are being led, the peace of God is out in front, leading you. When your peace leaves, you stop following. Do nothing else until your peace returns.

As an example, if someone asks you to do something that is wrong according God and man, you will have a visceral reaction. Your peace will leave, and anxiety will show up. Right then, you should say, "I have lost my peace, so I cannot do this or go any further in this direction." This is what it means to be led by the Spirit.

The second way you can be led by the Spirit is by heeding the Word of God as it pertains to that which you are preparing to do. In other words, follow what the Word of God says, and if the Word of God is not established by two or three witnesses, do not go past your peace.

> These things I have spoken unto you, that in me
> ye might have peace. In the world ye shall have
> tribulation: but be of good cheer; I have overcome
> the world. (John 16:33)

Having peace does not mean the absence of trouble. True peace reminds us that God is with us in the trouble and will deliver us from the trouble.

Jesus' disciples were in a storm, crossing the lake, but Jesus was sound asleep on a pillow in the rear of the boat.

> And he was in the hinder part of the ship, asleep
> on a pillow: and they awake him, and say unto
> him, Master, carest thou not that we perish?
> (Mark 4:38)

> Follow peace with all men, and holiness, without
> which no man shall see the Lord: God's word has
> and is speaking to believers all the time if they are
> reading his word and hearing his word.
> (Heb. 12:14)

We are to follow peace. We are not to go out on our own and wait for peace to show up.

When peace leaves, you ought to follow it. This does not mean to be a quitter. But when trouble shows up, do all that is within you to keep the peace. And then, watch God show up.

A WHOLE OTHER DOOR OPENS TO MAKE US SONS AND DAUGHTERS

The last part of Romans 8:14 says we are the "sons of God," meaning we now have sonship because we are being led by the Spirit of God. Wow! I can become God's son if I am led. Yes, you are now a son, and if you are a son, you have the rights of a son and not merely a servant. That's what the Bible says.

> If ye then, being evil, know how to give good gifts unto your children, how much more shall your Father which is in heaven give good things to them that ask him? (Matt. 7:11)

> If ye then, being evil, know how to give good gifts unto your children: how much more shall your heavenly Father give the Holy Spirit to them that ask him? (Matt. 11:13)

Therefore, knowing God is my Father, all I have to do is cry "Abba, Father", and He will do for me what He did for Jesus.

Jesus was led by the Spirit, so we too must be led by the Spirit. Jesus was led by the Word, so we too must be led by the Word.

In the story of the Prodigal Son, the son never experienced being treated as a servant. His father ran out to meet him. Before he could ask to become a servant, the father identified him as his son who had returned. For all intents and purposes, he had been dead but now was alive. They clothed him with a robe, put a ring on his finger, and killed the fatted calf to have a party for him.

> And the son said unto him, Father, I have sinned against heaven, and in thy sight, and am no more worthy to be called thy son. But the father said to his servants, Bring forth the best robe, and put it on him; and put a ring on his hand, and shoes on his feet: And bring hither the fatted calf, and kill it; and let us eat, and be merry: For this my son was dead, and is alive again; he was lost, and is found. And they began to be merry.
> (Luke 15:21-24)

When we are led by the Spirit, we are the sons and daughters of God.

> And if ye be Christ's, then are ye Abraham's seed, and heirs according to the promise. (Gal. 3:29)

I know it doesn't seem fair to be called a son of God after messing up so badly, but God has forgiven us of all our sins past, present, and future. Therefore, we are forgiven! And God is not holding anything against or back from us. We are his children. This is the grace of God in full action.

You're vulnerable if you don't know who is leading you

Chaos, confusion, and division will run wild when you don't know who is leading you.

All kinds of confusion was breaking out at the beginning of the evacuation. The mayor of the city was saying he was the leader and the person in control. The governor was saying she was the leader and the person in control. The head of FEMA, the Federal Emergency Management Agency team, was saying he was in control. As a result of all the chaos and confusion, people did not know who to follow. This led the people to do the wrong things. Some lost their lives as a result of poor leadership.

People were so divided they did not know if they could trust the first responders. No one knew if they were to stay or leave. If they could not leave, they didn't know where to go for refuge from the storm. Overall, it was bad. We watched people on rooftops calling for help and dead people covered by blankets outside of buildings used as places of refuge.

In the Bible, there were times when the children of Israel did not know who was leading them, and it brought confusion in the camp, but God made it clear who they were to follow from among the children of Israel.

> And the Lord spake suddenly unto Moses, and unto Aaron, and unto Miriam, Come out ye three unto the tabernacle of the congregation. And they three came out. And the Lord came down in the pillar of the cloud, and stood in the door of the tabernacle, and called Aaron and Miriam: and they both came forth. And he said, Hear now my words: If there be a prophet among you, I the Lord will make myself known unto him in a vision, and will speak unto him in a dream. My servant Moses is not so, who is faithful in all mine house. With him will I speak mouth to mouth, even apparently, and not in dark speeches; and the similitude of the Lord shall he behold: wherefore then were ye not afraid to speak against my servant Moses? (Num. 12:4-8)

When God is allowed to lead, you will know it

When God is allowed to lead, you will know it because where he leads he provides. Although God is not coming to earth in the flesh to lead us, He has chosen men and women to get the job done.

> Whosoever shall receive one of such children in my name, receiveth me: and whosoever shall receive me, receiveth not me, but him that sent me. (Mark 9:37)

> He that heareth you heareth me; and he that despiseth you despiseth me; and he that despiseth me despiseth him that sent me. (Luke 10:16)

God uses people here on earth to lead us. If we do not receive them, we are not rejecting the person but Jesus Himself. It is He who has made the choice. If we receive Him, we receive Jesus who sent Him.

If Jesus were to show up at our homes, no believer I know would dare not receive Him. Yet we refuse to receive some people who Jesus has sent to be His ambassadors in the earth. We know His ambassadors by the Word of God that is preached or taught. The peace of God follows His Word. So if you think someone is not being led by God to be the leader, check to see if you have any peace in your spirit. No peace, no action.

Group leaders must also remember that, if someone rejects what you are saying, they are not rejecting you but the One who sent you. In other words, don't take it personally. You are just the messenger. It is not your message, nor is it your responsibility to make it happen.

In my case, I had been given the role to lead the evacuees that were with us.

WHO IS LEADING YOU?

- Emotions?
- People and friends?
- Family traditions?
- Money or the lack thereof?
- The wrong authority?
- The news?
- A political party?
- Traditions?
- Superstitions?

When you know someone, it is because you have taken time to get to know him or her. When you know who it is who is leading you, it's because you have taken the time necessary to get to know that person. You cannot know someone without investing time, energy, and effort in the process. Likewise, we must make a true time investment in getting to know the Lord and His Word concerning how He wants to lead us.

Many people depend solely on someone else to do all the work so they can simply reap the benefits that follow. In order to be good followers, we must know God personally. At the point when we must be led, we not only can follow others who are in charge, but we can also hear from God ourselves.

> But ye believe not, because ye are not of my sheep, as I said unto you. My sheep hear my voice, and I know them, and they follow me: And I give unto them eternal life; and they shall never perish, neither shall any man pluck them out of my hand. (John 10:26-28)

> I am the good shepherd, and know my sheep, and am known of mine. (John 10:14)

People don't follow Him because they don't know Him. But when you know Him, it's because you follow Him and not another. People don't know Him because they do not believe in Him.

BELIEVE IN JESUS, AND GET TO KNOW HIM

We get to know Him in the following process. As we follow the Word of God, we get to know the Lord. He already knows us. We follow God in the little things, and more and more, we gain confidence in His Word and ways.

> He that is faithful in that which is least is faithful also in much: and he that is unjust in the least is unjust also in much. (Luke 16:10)

Chapter 3

Don't Murmur Against the Plan

A s I prepared to deliver the third session, I was impressed to caution those caught in transition not to murmur against the plan coming to help them. Neither should they murmur against the people in charge of administering the plan. There was a lot of confusion at the beginning of the evacuation process as to who was in charge. The mayor of the city was trying to exercise his authority. Likewise, the Lieutenant Governor, the Governor, and FEMA were all in a power struggle. Undoubtedly, everyone was trying to help the people in trouble, but so many messages were being put out that people began complaining about the message and the messengers.

The plan from God is always to bring us to a place of promise with nothing missing or broken.

> For I know the thoughts that I think toward you, saith the LORD, thoughts of peace, and not of evil, to give you an expected end. (Jer. 29:11)

If we murmur against the plan that God has for us, we can hinder both the execution and the timing of the plan. I believe the plan will be executed but the timing and success of the plan will be hampered. From Genesis to Revelation, God has always had a plan for man. But man's failure to carry out that plan has been catastrophic.

The plan for Adam and Eve was that they would live forever in the Garden of Eden. The plan for Abraham was that he would live in the blessing forever. The plan for David was that he would build a temple for the presence of the Lord. All of those plans changed.

I want to talk about the plan God had for Israel when they were delivered from Egypt. The plan was for them to be His people and for Him to supply them with everything they needed for the rest of their lives. On the way to executing this plan, they murmured about the plan and the person (Moses) who had been given the plan to get them where they were to go. Here are a few definitions of *murmur*: "to stay permanently; hence (in a bad sense) to be obstinate (especially in words, to complain): abide (all night), continue, dwell, endure, grudge, be left, lie all night, (cause to) lodge (all night, in, ing, this night), (make to) murmur, remain, tarry (all night, that night)." And such was exactly what some people were doing before the storm. They were murmuring about staying put right where they were, "come hell or high water." Well, hell and high water were on their way. Water doesn't ask for permission to come. When enough of it swells in the right place, it will go wherever it has the force to flow. Murmuring does not fix the problem. If anything, it makes the problem worse because the problem now has become the murmuring.

The greatest thing about all of these examples of people murmuring is that God still blessed them in the end, and no amount of negative talk changed God's mind about blessing His people. This truth alone should be enough to make you want to shout, "Thank You, Father, for blessing me!" Right now, raise your hands and say, "Thank You, Lord! Thank You for all that You have done and all that You will do in my life!"

HAST THOU TAKEN US AWAY TO DIE IN THE WILDERNESS?

> And they said unto Moses, Because there were no graves in Egypt, hast thou taken us away to die in the wilderness? wherefore hast thou dealt thus with us, to carry us forth out of Egypt?
> (Ex. 14:11)

They began murmuring about the plan to leave Egypt right from the beginning. We must remember or understand that, when

God gives plans to man, He doesn't give the whole plan at once. I believe this is because we would run ahead of God in our own efforts and make a mess of the plan.

There was certainly a mess made of the plans given to evacuate the city before the great storm hit. You have seen people get in trouble by letting pieces of a plan out before its time. Nothing good has ever come from premature actions.

As you are moving from one place to another in this transition due to the storm, remember not to get ahead of the planners. Don't open the test before you have heard all of the instructions. In school, when the teacher said to listen to all of the instructions before beginning the test, I hope you were not one of the people who missed the instruction of putting your name on the exam and, when the exam was over, you did not pass because your name was not on your exam.

God is not like the world. He does not give exams for us to fail, but He gives exams to show us where we are in God. The people of Israel murmured constantly about the plan to move them into the Promised Land. It only slowed them down, and some died because of not following the plan. The entire time they were in the wilderness, God provided for them: water, manna from heaven, meat, and no sickness. Their shoes and clothes did not wear out. This is the kind of God we serve, a never-ending supply. He is not a mean God who is looking to punish you every time you miss the mark.

THE PLAN IS NOT THE PROBLEM

Some of the Israelites had a problem with the plan because it led them to the Red Sea with what looked like no escape for them. God will never lead us to a dead end or to a place of no escape.

> There hath no temptation taken you but such as is common to man: but God is faithful, who will not suffer you to be tempted above that ye are able; but will with the temptation also make a way to escape, that ye may be able to bear it.
> (1 Cor. 10:13)

God's plan was to have Israel go forward into the Promised Land and destroy their enemies that were following them to bring them back into slavery.

> And Moses said unto the people, Fear ye not, stand still, and see the salvation of the Lord, which he will shew to you today: for the Egyptians whom ye have seen today, ye shall see them again no more forever. (Ex. 14:13)

Some of the things people saw as enemies when they evacuated the Gulf Coast they would see no more. The plan was not the problem for the city. It was people not following the instructions, people not having the resources to follow the instructions, and the execution of the plan. Consequently, people were left stranded and abandoned to fend for themselves in the greatest disaster in history of the state, but God had another plan

> For I know the thoughts that I think toward you,
> saith the Lord, thoughts of peace, and not of evil,
> to give you an expected end. (Jer. 29:11)

God's plan has an expected end, one that is good and not bad. So follow the plan of God.

THE PERSON WITH THE PLAN IS NOT THE PROBLEM

God uses people to carry out his plans, so we should not get caught up in worrying about who the person is leading the plan. Never mind the package the plan comes in, just take the plan and execute as instructed.

In our society, we sometimes have issues with gender, race, and or ethnicity. As in the case of this emergency, we had an African-American mayor, a female Governor, and a male in charge of FEMA. I believe some people had trouble with trusting a female in the Governor's office. People had mixed feelings about who to believe and who to trust because they did not like the package from which the plan disseminated.

The same thing happened to Moses in leading the children of Israel. They had issue with Moses having a wife of color being the leader of them, but God had no issues with it. God uses people to carry out his plan regardless of the package.

> Turn you at my reproof: behold, I will pour out my spirit unto you, I will make known my words unto you. (Prov. 1:23)

"I will pour out my Spirit on you" means all of us and not just men, women, blacks, or whites but on whoever believes.

> For the promise is unto you, and to your children, and to all that are afar off, as many as the Lord our God shall call. (Acts 2:29)

Moses was a runaway prince of Egypt turned slave. He was also a murderer who had killed a man before fleeing Egypt. However, God had no issues with Moses because he was forgiven and chosen by God, and gifts and callings are "without repentance" (Rom. 11:29).

Jesus said for us not to get angry or take it personally when someone does not receive the message He gave to us to deliver. They are not rejecting the messenger but God who gave the plan. Remember you are only the messenger. Whenever you focus on people, you will lose the message. People are not perfect, but God who gave the plan to help you knows what's best for you.

THE PLAN COMES WITH BENEFITS NOT ALWAYS SEEN

During the aftermath of this great storm, people were benefiting from the disaster relief that comes when people are displaced by a major catastrophe. There were insurance benefits, low-cost loans, temporary shelters, long-term shelters, and all kinds of resources made available to people because of the devastation and loss.

Likewise, for the believer, there are all kinds of benefits for following the plan of God. Earlier, we saw that the Israelites had protection and guidance.

> And the Lord went before them by day in a pillar of a cloud, to lead them the way; and by night in a pillar of fire, to give them light; to go by day and night: He took not away the pillar of the cloud by day, nor the pillar of fire by night, from before the people. (Ex. 13:21-22)

God's plan had no-cost insurance for everyone because they did not suffer from sickness or disease during their Exodus from Egypt. Child of God, what I am saying is there are benefits for being the people of God. Here are some of the benefits from God:

GOD ALWAYS FORGIVES US AND NEVER HOLDS ANYTHING AGAINST US

> For I will be merciful to their unrighteousness, and their sins and their iniquities will I remember no more. (Heb. 8:12)

> As far as the east is from the west, so far hath he removed our transgressions from us. (Psa. 103:12)

GOD LOVES US

> But God commendeth his love toward us, in that, while we were yet sinners, Christ died for us. (Rom. 5:8)

GOD GIVES US A NEVER-ENDING SUPPLY

> But my God shall supply all your need according to his riches in glory by Christ Jesus. (Phil. 4:19) And God is able to make all grace abound toward you; that ye, always having all sufficiency in all things, may abound to every good work: (As it is

written, He hath dispersed abroad; he hath given to the poor: his righteousness remaineth forever. Now he that ministereth seed to the sower both minister bread for your food, and multiply your seed sown, and increase the fruits of your righteousness;) Being enriched in everything to all bountifulness, which causeth through us thanksgiving to God. (2 Cor. 9:8-11)

GOD HEALS US

But he was wounded for our transgressions, he was bruised for our iniquities: the chastisement of our peace was upon him; and with his stripes we are healed. (Isa. 53:5)

Who his own self bare our sins in his own body on the tree that we, being dead to sins, should live unto righteousness: by whose stripes ye were healed. (1 Pet. 2:24)

GOD PROTECTS US FROM ALL DESTRUCTION

God is our refuge and strength, a very present help in trouble. Therefore will not we fear, though the earth be removed, and though the mountains be carried into the midst of the sea; Though the waters thereof roar and be troubled, though the mountains shake with the swelling thereof. Selah. There is a river, the streams whereof shall make glad the city of God, the holy place of the tabernacles of the most High. God is in the midst of her; she shall not be moved: God shall help her, and that right early. (Psa. 46:1-5)

The LORD is nigh unto all them that call upon him, to all that call upon him in truth.
(Psa. 145:18)

FOLLOW THE INSTRUCTIONS TO THE LETTER

Have you ever attempted to assemble something or repair something that came with a set of instructions, but for some strange reason, you decided not to follow all of the instructions? You had this overwhelming desire to assemble this equipment or complete this task off of the old, traditional methods of, "I have done things like this a thousand times. This is the way we have always done it." Sound familiar? Just when you thought you had it all done, you find out that one step or one part you left out was critical to the operation of the whole thing, so you had to disassemble the whole thing and start over.

The same goes for following the instructions given by God. We must follow them exactly the way they were given, or we will not see the kinds of results desired or promised.

> And it shall come to pass, if thou shalt hearken diligently unto the voice of the Lord thy God, to observe and to do all his commandments which I command thee this day, that the Lord thy God will set thee on high above all nations of the earth: And all these blessings shall come on thee, and overtake thee, if thou shalt hearken unto the voice of the Lord thy God. Blessed shalt thou be in the city, and blessed shalt thou be in the field. (Deut. 28:1-3)

Partial obedience is considered no obedience in the secular world and in the Word of God. Follow the instruction as if your life depended on it.

When we said "follow all of the instructions" to the evacuees, I could hear a collective gasp and panic attack from the room. I have had the same feelings, and I believe it comes from thinking there is no way I will be able to do all that the Word of God says to be blessed. Good news! God is not asking us to act upon every scripture in the Bible right now. The reason He is not asking us to act upon all the scripture in the Bible is because

Jesus has already paid it all for us at the cross of Calvary. I also believe it is a trick from the Enemy to cause people to feel overwhelmed in catastrophes, trying to get them to believe they have to cross every "t" and dot every "i" before God will deliver or help. It is simply not true.

God is a God of grace, mercy, and forgiveness. He does not wait for us to do anything because His mercy and kindness are forever in motion. We have His Word on that. God gave His only begotten Son. God does not lie.

> God is not a man, that he should lie; neither the son of man, that he should repent: hath he said, and shall he not do it? or hath he spoken, and shall he not make it good? (Num. 23:19)

We live in a fallen world where men can lie and renege on promises, but God will never lie because He simply cannot lie. Though men lie, God will make good on His Word in all areas.

> And we know that all things work together for good to them that love God, to them who are the called according to his purpose. (Rom. 8:26)

I don't know how God does it, but He makes all things new and better and works all things out for our good.

REVELATIONS COMES WITH THE PLAN

Whenever we follow the plan of God, He provides one revelation after another.

God reveals His plan to believers and does not keep anything from those who believe. I know you have heard it said God works in mysterious ways, but He does not keep them a mystery to the saints.

> But God hath revealed them unto us by his Spirit: for the Spirit searcheth all things, yea, the deep things of God. (1 Cor. 2:10)

Joseph, who was sold into slavery by his brothers, was given a dream from God—a plan, if you will—that would eventually come to pass and be instrumental in saving his entire family. As you read Joseph's story all the way from where his brothers threw him into a pit to Pharaoh's palace where he was second-in-command, God revealed to him wisdom and interpretations of dreams with the ability to save his family.

Revelation comes with the plan. Warning comes before destruction. We may not always see the warning signs, but they do come.

Pride goeth before destruction, and an haughty spirit before a fall. (Prov. 16:18)

GOD WANTS US TO KNOW ALL THINGS

If ye have heard of the dispensation of the grace of God which is given me to youward: How that by revelation he made known unto me the mystery; (as I wrote afore in few words, Whereby, when ye read, ye may understand my knowledge in the mystery of Christ). (Eph. 3:2-4)

Even the mystery which hath been hid from ages and from generations, but now is made manifest to his saints: To whom God would make known what is the riches of the glory of this mystery among the Gentiles; which is Christ in you, the hope of glory. (Col. 1:26-27)

God is not keeping anything back from His saints.

MURMURING SLOWS DOWN THE PLAN AND YOU

During the evacuation, many people tried to wait for the so-called best time to leave, but it was the wrong time in almost every case. Even my family members waited too long before evacuating, and it took them 12 hours to drive what would have otherwise been a three-hour drive if they had followed instructions. The highways were jammed and resembled a massive parking lot, moving an inch at a time. People had to be plucked from the highway due to running out of fuel.

When the plan slows down, you slow down because now many people are involved, and it takes time to get the message to everyone. The plan slows down when too many people are trying to debate the right thing to do and too many opinions have entered into the plan.

There were over three million Israelites exiting from Egypt. If you were to stop and have a town hall meeting to find out when to leave, they would have hardly made it outside the city limit. There needed to be a single voice of communication.

Remember the school game the teachers had us play to emphasize the importance of good communication? The game consisted of one piece of information being whispered from one person to the next in a chain of multiple people. The person at the end of the line would try to repeat the message as accurately as possible. The message would always be totally different by the time it had passed through everyone in the communication chain. This game illustrates why we need one line of communication during times of transition.

It should have taken only 11 days for the children of Israel to get to the Promised Land, but because of their murmuring, they spent 40 years wondering in the desert.

Because of the grace of God, we do not have to wander in the desert of our thinking. We just have to follow God's plan and be saved. I asked God why He took them on the route He did. I saw my answer in the scriptures.

> And it came to pass, when Pharaoh had let the people go, that God led them not through the way of the land of the Philistines, although that was near; for God said, Lest peradventure the people repent when they see war, and they return to Egypt: But God led the people about, through the way of the wilderness of the Red sea: and the children of Israel went up harnessed out of the land of Egypt. (Ex. 13:17-18)

The people had never seen war or trouble like they were going to see as they possessed the land God had for them. So God literally put them through school, so to speak, to train them and teach them how to depend on Him for everything.

Sometimes, a storm can cause you to remember who you are supposed to be depending on. That is not to say God sent the storm but that it is being used by Him in many ways.

Don't take it personal

This is for the leaders or the people who find themselves responsible for giving the plan. When people murmur, they are not murmuring against you, so don't take it personal. They are murmuring against the one who gave the plan, and that never works out.

You cannot murmur against the company you are working for or the boss you have because they are positioned in your life to be a blessing if you will respond in a godly way. If people God has placed in your life to help you get to the place He has planned refuse, the Lord will deal with them.

> But if the watchman see the sword come, and blow not the trumpet, and the people be not warned; if the sword come, and take any person from among them, he is taken away in his iniquity; but his blood will I require at the watchman's hand. (Ezek. 33:6)

The men and women of God who are used to help must do what they are told by the Lord, for they will be held accountable.

You can't murmur against your own house or against your spouse because that will hinder your prayers and your ability to be effective in the Kingdom of God. It will hinder your communication with the Lord.

> Every wise woman buildeth her house: but the
> foolish plucketh it down with her hands.
> (Prov. 14:1)

If you are wise, you will do everything in your power to build your own house and avoid everything that can tear it down.

God always has a better plan, and He uses people to carry out the plan. God is not coming to earth to carry out His plans for us. God uses people to carry out His plans on earth. For example, the story of the rich man and Lazarus ended with the rich man wanting to go back to earth from Hell to tell his brothers not to make the mistake he did of not helping people.

> Abraham saith unto him, They have Moses and
> the prophets; let them hear them. (Luke 16:29)

He received a response, and it was that they have the Bible and the men and women of God, people God has set aside to help us in the Word.

> How then shall they call on him in whom they
> have not believed? and how shall they believe in
> him of whom they have not heard? and how shall
> they hear without a preacher? And how shall they

preach, except they be sent? as it is written, How beautiful are the feet of them that preach the gospel of peace, and bring glad tidings of good things! (Rom. 10:14-15)

God uses people to help us. He is not going to override His established plan of preaching the gospel and the Word of God. God wants to help us through people. That is why it is so important to treat people right; you do not know who God is trying help through you.

CHOOSE NOT TO MURMUR

I remember this like it was yesterday. I had received one of the best performance reviews ever and, on top of that, a large raise. Shortly after that, the company began to have financial problems and decided to downsize its engineering and management personnel by 40 percent. They hired a new HR director who was known for his no-nonsense, take-no-prisoners approach to downsizing, and he began immediately cutting the workforce on all levels. I was moved to several areas of the local facility and remained in the company as a supervisor because I had high reviews and was well-liked by many.

After exhausting all avenues, the time came when the company approached me, and I was laid off. They continued to pay 90 percent of my salary for six months and then approached me with a buy-out package, which was very good. I turned down the buy-out package and reluctantly received an opportunity to be reassigned to another division in the company out of state with the hope and belief that I would be able to return at some point.

I was single at the time and felt I could tolerate and accept the move and be back at this location shortly. I moved to a cold-weather state. My plan was to get in, perform really well, and get out as quickly as possible. Plans will change!

After arriving at the new location, I found out that the winter there was so harsh that people had cars called "beaters" simply to avoid the wear and tear inflicted by the ice and salt on their good vehicles. The weather person reported one day that there had only been 13 days of sunshine the previous year, and the current year was not looking much better. The winter lasted for seven months, and July was the only summer month before the weather began to get cold again. I asked the company I was renting from for permission to paint all the rooms white because the cloudy conditions were making me depressed.

I began to see my situation as all bad. I started griping and complaining about the weather, not knowing anyone, and being miserable in that place. I vowed not to like it or to stay any longer than I had to. I was an unhappy individual most of the time, and I kept this up for two or three years. Yes, yours truly, the born-again Christian, was murmuring and complaining most of the time. I likened myself to being on the backside of the desert with sheep, and no one cared.

One day, in prayer, I began to ask God why He seemed to be ignoring my prayers. After all, I had been doing a great job. I heard so clearly by the Spirit,

> Son, I am not going to hear you until you stop complaining about the place you are in. Until you begin to appreciate the portion you have right now and be grateful for the place you are in right now, I will not hear you.

You have to understand I was sour about being in that state. To prove my displeasure about being there, I refused to unpack all of my household goods and left most of them in storage, vowing to get out of that place as fast as I could. I only unpacked the bare necessities: one chair, one plate, one fork, one cup...

When I heard what the Spirit said, I immediately repented and began to change the way I saw where I lived. I moved into a larger place, unpacked everything, and began to verbalize how I loved and appreciated the area, the job, and the people around me. When I changed, the people around me changed, and my life changed. I found winter sports I could get involved with and a ministry I could commit to. Life became so much better.

Here is the grand revelation and miracle from my newfound understanding of transition. I had a choice in all of it, and when I chose to stop murmuring, everything around me changed. Best of all, about six months after this epiphany and paradigm shift, my old plant called and said they could take me back if I wanted to return.

I remember the joy and excitement of being able to return to the place I was making home and one glaring, "ah ha" moment. I remember saying to the Lord, "Do you mean to tell me, if I had not murmured and stopped all my complaining years ago, I could have gotten this call to return before now?"

I heard, "Yes."

CHAPTER 4

PLANS CHANGE

It has been said that people are creatures of habit; they like for things to stay the same in order for life to make sense. People are naturally resistant to change because it can be disconcerting to have things change just when you think you're getting settled.

Several times in my professional career, I have had the unpleasant opportunity to have to change in areas of responsibility. It was unexpected and unwanted. I had to move from an active floor, managing processes and people, to a planning and administration position, which was totally out of my comfort zone. At first, I resisted everything about the move until one of my mentors explained to me that things change and work out for the best when we cooperate with the change rather than resisting. My mentor went on to explain that the change was really in the path I needed to be promoted in the area I was working because planning is a key component of the next level. Indeed, the change brought along a promotion for me a few years down the line.

Sometimes, you may not see the need for the change, but if you cooperate with the change, you can use the lessons learned to reach the next level of life or whatever you are pursuing. People plan their whole lives what they think should be done to have a better life only to find out as life progresses that plans change. The reason plans change is because life is dynamic and not static. Things in life are ever changing. Knowing that life is dynamic, we need to be flexible and accepting of the changes it brings.

Some people affected by Hurricane Katrina were just getting settled in when the storm changed their plans. Isn't that just like life? You plan for everything you can think of, and then something you did not plan for happens and causes you to change your plans.

When you look back over time, things have always changed. We just did not make note of all the changes or when the changes were occurring. For example, the educational system in America has changed significantly. There used to be a time in America when it was acceptable to only finish a certain level of schooling, and no one would fuss over only finishing middle school. Not anymore. Today, a college education has become the norm.

Israel had a plan. They wanted to come out of bondage and directly into the Promised Land, but God had another plan. Sometimes, plans have to be changed to adjust to the needs of people and their environment.

I have discovered personally that, when I am flexible to plans for me and others, things go smoother and more effectively. This is not to say there will not be any problems, but being flexible and having an open mind to changes has helped tremendously in making adjustments when plans change. At the same time, I have caused many problems, delays, economical losses, and setbacks for myself by being resistant to plans changing.

During my first years of being employed with a Fortune 500 company, I refused to make adjustments from critiques about my job performance from superiors unless they could prove they had used the same criteria with everyone else. To make a long story short, I was passed over for promotions until I began to make the adjustments needed to make it to the next level. As I look at it now, it was all in my control to make the adjustments.

GOD HAS ANOTHER PLAN

The children of Israel could have easily crossed through the land of the Philistines to get to the Promised Land in just 11 days, but God had another plan for Israel.

> But God led the people about, through the way of the wilderness of the Red sea: and the children of Israel went up harnessed out of the land of Egypt. (Ex. 13:18)

God knows what's best for us even though we can't see the entire plan. At this time in this history of Israel, they only knew how to be slaves, servants, and people who had no real knowledge of how to function apart from taskmasters telling them what to do. When you do not know what to do, someone has to teach you what to do. You cannot do what you do not know. When you know what to do, it becomes more likely that you can and will do what is needed. In the corporate world, I have found this to be true, time and time again. When people know what to do, they excel and are much more proficient and successful in accomplishing the task with great quality and pride.

God's plan was simple and would have been highly effective if it would have been received by the people without murmuring. His plan was to establish with the people that He was their Source in life. So many times after their murmuring, God provided, and they were able to move on. The pattern of God providing everything they needed should have been caught after so many times, but it wasn't. Israel missed it. Because they missed it, they wandered in the desert for 40 years before God decided they had learned their lesson.

> Your carcasses shall fall in this wilderness; and all
> that were numbered of you, according to your
> whole number, from twenty years old and upward,

which have murmured against me, Doubtless ye shall not come into the land, concerning which I sware to make you dwell therein, save Caleb the son of Jephunneh, and Joshua the son of Nun. (Num. 14:29-30)

So many people missed the plan when trying to evacuate from Hurricane Katrina because they did not know what to do.

THE PEOPLE HAD ONE PLAN, BUT GOD HAD ANOTHER PLAN

I have found in my life that my plans must look funny in God's sight because everything I have ever planned changed, and it was for the best. It has been said that, if you want to make God laugh, show Him your plans.

I studied to be an electronic design engineer for four years, but when I graduated from college, I could sense God moving me in another direction. My first job was as a supervisor for a major manufacturing company, managing people and equipment, something I had never been trained to do. My second job was more change because I went from managing 30 people to 300 people, seven supervisors, and a multi-million dollar facility. My schooling had not prepared me for these challenges.

I thought this would have been the end of plans changing, but several more came over the next 30 years. They were not all smooth, but I was able to make the change far better by understanding that plans change and that I need to be flexible and open to change. Yes, there were some times when I resisted, but I soon gave in to what God was doing in my life.

After seeing plans change so many times, I can tell you it's all good. My last change in the corporate world was coming when I had received a promotion. I began to plan my next move for a few years later. I had a great performance review, and the manager from the next area approached me and confirmed I was on track to make the next move up with a large raise. I was excited and could see financial and personal success.

During prayer time one day, I heard by the Spirit, "I have another plan for Lance." I was curious to hear but anxious at the same time because I did not want my plans to change. I heard clearly by the Spirit, "I want you to go into full-time ministry soon." I was okay with that because I thought it would be in the city of my choice, but it was not. I also heard, "I want you to go south and begin ministry." Immediately, I had mixed emotions, knowing I would have to let my own plans go and follow the plan God had.

It was difficult, and I made some mistakes just like the children of Israel did by complaining and wanting to do things my way. After all was said and done, I followed the plan of God, and it was a miracle how He put us in the South at no cost to us, moving to two cities on our way south. God provided every dime we needed and opened every door we needed to have open to get us to the place where we are now.

Where there is a vision from the Lord, there is provision. We have not lacked anything since both my wife and I quit our jobs and went full time in the ministry. Things have been tight financially a couple of times, but we have never run out or been in any lack following God. I had to take a job one time for three years to supplement our income, but God opened the door for the work that led to a huge blessing for us and several other ministries. The door God opened was with the company I resigned from that said I could never come back under any condition after resigning. They called me to come back, and I reminded them of the terms of the agreement.

They said, "Never mind what we said. We need you to help us. Will you come back for a short while?"

I agreed to come back for six months, which turned into three years. Here is the huge blessing. The company allowed me to have any and everything I needed for the ministry concerning equipment and said I could also be a blessing by getting things for other ministries in town. We summarized the list of equipment acquired, and it came to several hundred thousands of dollars. We were able to give five other churches equipment still under warranty with supplies for free.

But wait… There is more. I received a voucher for working there the last day by the local workforce to go back to school because the plant shut down. The education voucher allowed me to get a master's degree and PhD in Christian Counseling that not only helps the ministry but also the people in the community.

God had another plan for my life, and it is all good. There are so many more plans I could tell you about, but we will move forward. We are now in full-time ministry, and I have a thriving pastoral and community counseling service now that is a blessing to the city and the surrounding areas.

You will never lose following the plan of God. Remember to be open to change when God's plan changes. After all, it is His plan, and He is able to give us what we need to get His plan done.

> Now unto him that is able to do exceeding abundantly above all that we ask or think, according to the power that worketh in us…
> (Eph. 3:20)

The power is in us to change, and there is more power in us than we realize. Everything must change. Nothing stays the same on earth. The only thing that is the same on planet Earth is God's love, grace, and mercy for humanity.

Jesus Christ the same yesterday, and today, and forever. (Heb. 13:8)

Another example of how plans change is the life of the Apostle Paul. He started out as a scholar and keeper of the law who persecuted Christians. Saul met the Lord on the road to Damascus, and his life changed forever. No doubt, Saul who later was called Paul thought his life would always be Saul the persecutor, but God had another plan for Saul's life.

His change did not happen overnight. And much like Paul's life, if we are going to experience lasting change, we need to know it comes through a process of time. For example, Paul spent several years under the mentorship of Barnabas before going into full-time ministry as he was called to do. The time was over 14 years from when he began his relationship with Jesus on the road to Damascus. If I had to wait 14 years, I probably would have given up, but Paul remained faithful to Barnabas until a dispute arose over what direction they would go and who would go with them.

And the contention was so sharp between them, that they departed asunder one from the other: and so Barnabas took Mark, and sailed unto Cyprus; And Paul chose Silas, and departed, being recommended by the brethren unto the grace of God. (Acts 15:39-40)

I could see the frustration on the faces of the people who were living with us that evacuated. They were ready to return home. It's not easy leaving everything you own behind and not knowing what has become of it, but when you have God's Word concerning your situation, everything will work out well for you.

And we know that all things work together for good to them that love God, to them who are the called according to his purpose. (Rom. 8:28)

SAUL FLOWED WITH THE CHANGE

In order to flow with changes, we have to line up with the plan and the Word of God and go in the same direction.

Can two walk together, except they be agreed? (Amos 3:3)

We have to agree with the plan and line up with the plan even if we cannot see the entire plan at once. When we agree with a plan, it is not that we are saying the plan is perfect but that, for the sake of progressing toward our destination, we are on the same page with the direction. You may not like it, but you must agree to follow the plan to walk in agreement.

People walking in different directions will never get to their desired destinations. The Enemy likes to bring confusion and chaos to stop progress and to destroy the plan.

THE LORD EMPOWERED HIM TO CHANGE

Pray for the same empowerment Paul received to carry out the plan of God, and you will be successful as Paul was. God gives to us the ability to do what is required, and that ability is called the grace of God. God will grace you to do what needs to be done when you yield to the plan.

> But by the grace of God I am what I am: and his grace which was bestowed upon me was not in vain; but I laboured more abundantly than they all: yet not I, but the grace of God which was with me. (1 Cor. 15:10)

We are all given a measure of faith whereby we access the grace of God to do what is required. So many times, I have wondered how to accomplish what God asked of me. And every time, I was able to get it done because of the grace of God. I received the knowledge to get it done, or a person with the knowledge came into my life at the right time to share with me what needed to be done. God is a keeper of His Word, and He said He would never leave us or forsake us.

> Be strong and of a good courage, fear not, nor be afraid of them: for the Lord thy God, he it is that doth go with thee; he will not fail thee, nor forsake thee. (Deut. 31:6)

> What shall we then say to these things? If God be for us, who can be against us? (Rom. 8:31)

I know Joseph had to say more than once to himself that his circumstances did not look like they were part of God's plan for him to save his family. But God was with him to empower him to make it through every trial.

Joseph went through some stuff, and you may have to go through some stuff. But go through. Don't stop.

Today, people don't want to go through anything. They just want it to be over and done with. The problem is nothing will be learned if you don't complete the journey.

THE CHANGE HELPED HIM AND OTHERS

In the story of Joseph, the dream was given to help him and others. Many times, people will lose sight of the opportunity for others to be blessed while they are in the midst of a trial or test. It can be easy to see how this would happen when everything you have worked and lived for is going to be washed away by a storm. But if you can gather yourself as Joseph had to, you will see that it is not about you but about God bringing His will to pass. The best thing about it is God never forgets about us while others are being helped.

> For God is not unrighteous to forget your work and labour of love, which ye have shewed toward his name, in that ye have ministered to the saints, and do minister. (Heb. 6:10)

Do not allow the enemy to cause you to focus on yourself when plans change.

People can forget sometimes. For example, maybe you have loaned money to someone who forgot to pay you back. But God never forgets. Memory capacity seems to be built into everyone, but forgetting takes effort. We must purposely forget about what is in it for us and say, "Nevertheless, Lord, Your will be done."

THANK GOD FOR THE CHANGE

It may be difficult for you to thank God for the changes happening in your life, but I know you can do it. Be thankful for wherever you find yourself. Be grateful for your portion. The voice of thanksgiving gets God involved.

> Not that I speak in respect of want: for I have learned, in whatsoever state I am, therewith to be content. I know both how to be abased, and I know how to abound: everywhere and in all things I am instructed both to be full and to be hungry, both to abound and to suffer need. I can do all things through Christ which strengtheneth me. (Phil. 4:11-13)

Christ, the Anointed One, has made His anointing available to us through His death, burial, and resurrection so we can do all things. Make being thankful an automatic reaction. In other words, train yourself to be thankful, and you will be thankful.

How can we train ourselves to be thankful? Use the Word of God. Say it out aloud with your mouth and in your heart, and it will take root and flourish, bringing a multiplied harvest of your needs being met with much more to put in store. Being thankful doesn't require any particular financial status. Just verbalize your gratitude, and when you hear it, your faith will increase.

UNDERSTAND PLANS CHANGE, BUT GOD DOES NOT

Plans will change, but understand God does not change.

> Jesus Christ the same yesterday, and today, and
> forever. (Heb. 13:8)

It's easy to remember Jesus is the same yesterday because we know He died for us over 2,000 years ago, and easy to remember he is the same today because we woke up this morning and are breathing air. But when it comes to believing and knowing He is the same forever, our faith begins to get shaky.

Yet, before we were born, Jesus died for us over 2,000 years ago. Two thousand years ago, today was the future, and God was already providing for us. Jesus is not going to be sacrificed again for our sins; it is a finished work forever.

> By the which will we are sanctified through the
> offering of the body of Jesus Christ once for all.
> (Heb. 10:10)

Where I grew up, "once for all" means forever. Forever is forever, and that means He plans on taking care of us even in the future. It is settled. God is for me forever.

> Forever, O Lord, thy word is settled in heaven.
> Thy faithfulness is unto all generations: thou hast
> established the earth, and it abideth. They

continue this day according to thine ordinances: for all are thy servants. (Ps. 119:89-91)

He hath remembered his covenant forever, the word which he commanded to a thousand generations. (Ps. 105:8)

That covers it.

ACCEPT WHAT GOD ALLOWS

Here are a few reminders…

Get in the flow. Walk in agreement with the Word and the plan.

God empowers us to get it done. It's not our battle but the Lord's.

Be thankful for the portion you have, and know it's not all about you.

Others will be helped, so train yourself to be thankful.

God never forgets.

God is the same yesterday, today, and forever

God has so many ways to deliver us. We cannot get stuck on a certain method or plan that worked in the past because He is always doing new things for His people. Look at these scriptures:

Behold, I will do a new thing; now it shall spring forth; shall ye not know it? I will even make a way in the wilderness, and rivers in the desert. (Isa. 43:19)

Thou hast heard, see all this; and will not ye declare it? I have shewed thee new things from this time, even hidden things, and thou didst not know them. (Isa. 48:6)

Behold ye among the heathen, and regard, and wonder marvelously: for I will work a work in your days, which ye will not believe, though it be told you. (Hab. 1:5)

Look at the children of Israel. They had been delivered so many times from the hand of the enemy, plagues, giants, and more. Don't settle for the old. Keep looking for God to bring you out, and remember that He has more ways out than we know of.

CHANGE IS NOT CHANGE UNTIL YOU CHANGE

So many times, people want someone else to change.

"Lord, if You would make them do this, I will do that."

"Lord, if they would just stop doing things to irritate me, I would be able to keep my temper."

How about you change what you are doing to get irritated. How about you stop allowing others to dictate how you respond. No one should be able to make another person do anything. We can only control what or how we respond and can never control anyone else. Change is not change until *you* change because we have no power over anyone else. We only have power over ourselves.

I have personally found out that, if I change what is under my control and do not try to change others, people and things around me begin to change. People started seeing the change because I began to submit to others more and regard others as imperfect just as I was imperfect.

Change starts with you… never the other person. Somebody has to get it started. Why not you?

Once I found out what to do, I started doing it, little by little and piece by piece. Don't try to change everything at once; that could lead to disastrous results. Take one thing at a time, and check your environment and people you trust to see if that one thing you changed is working. Then, go to the next thing.

WHEN PEOPLE KNOW WHAT TO DO THEY CAN DO IT

God will always tell us what He wants to do and will not have us in the dark about His plan for us. The worst thing that can happen for people is to not know God's plan for them. I am not talking about knowing the company's plan or your insurance plan. I am talking about God's plan for your life. God will not have you ignorant about what He wants you to do. So, take time to ask God, "What is your plan for my life?" He will reveal it to you.

When you know what to do, you'll start learning how to do it effectively and correctly. Biblical training is vital. *Train* means to give them a taste of instruction, little by little. Instructions should be simple, short, safe, and accurate. Wrong and inaccurate training leads to inaccurate results and often failure. This is why being in a great, Bible-believing and Bible-teaching church is critical. They can teach you according to the Word of God what to do, and then you will be able to accomplish your plan in life according to the scriptures.

Because a great majority of people who evacuated from Hurricane Katrina were confused and did not know what to do, some perished, and many were stranded for days without help. God will never leave us stranded or without help.

> Let your conversation be without covetousness; and be content with such things as ye have: for he hath said, I will never leave thee, nor forsake thee. (Heb. 13:5)

EVERY SEASON OF LIFE HAS A PLAN

Every season of life has a plan, and you must recognize what season of life you are in and the plan for that season. I used this football analogy to describe life seasons in this teaching. Life is like four quarters of football. In the first quarter as a 17-year-old, we try every play in the book and some not in the book to see which will be successful because we feel like we have the time and energy to do so.

In the second quarter of life from 17-34, we stop trying everything and begin to use what works, but we still aren't in a hurry.

We go into halftime and review what we've done by 34, throw out all that is not working, and begin to hone in on what works.

Then, we come out of the halftime charged up and ready to make the best run at doing the right things. In the third quarter from 34-51, there are no more trick plays or gimmicks. We're doing everything we can to win.

When you get to the fourth quarter from 51-68, you begin to hold onto what you have gained and strategically look to invest, advance, and win the game. You don't need as much as you once thought, and you desire to be a blessing to your family and to those around you.

You must know what season you are in. When I was young, I could run all day and do things without thinking about them. However, in the fourth quarter of life, I can't run all day and cannot afford to act without thinking the whole plan through. Life changes. Plans change. But God never changes. He is the same yesterday, today, and forevermore. That is why I put my trust in God and my focus on God. That is why my hearing is tuned into God. The plan may change, but God still knows how to lead us and guide us through everything in life. A storm may blow in off the coast of life and change the plan, but God who knows the plans and thoughts concerning us will bring us to an expected end. He will cause us to be able to adjust to the new plan.

> For I know the thoughts that I think toward you, saith the LORD, thoughts of peace, and not of evil, to give you an expected end. (Jer. 29:11)

> My substance was not hid from thee, when I was made in secret, and curiously wrought in the lowest parts of the earth. Thine eyes did see my substance, yet being unperfect; and in thy book all my members were written, which in continuance

were fashioned, when as yet there was none of them. (Ps. 139:15-16)

God knew before we were born the plans He had for us. In His book, all my members were written. In other words, everything I need to know about me and how to navigate through life can be found in the Word of God.

CHAPTER 5

KNOW THE WILL OF GOD FOR YOUR LIFE

I felt pushed for time to get as much information out that would be helpful to the people of God that evacuated from Hurricane Katrina. I taught on the subject of knowing the will of God. They were hanging onto every word for the last few sessions, so I prayed for wisdom to have simple and short examples. I have seen entire books written about how to know the will of God, but this will be short and to the point.

The will of God is the Word of God, and His Word is His will. Let's define the word *will*.

> Will / thelema (thel'-ay-mah): A determination; Decree; Desire, pleasure, choice, often referring to God's "preferred-will."

It was God's determination to save man and bring man back into right relationship with Him, and a decree was made to send His Son, Jesus, into the world as the sacrifice for man. It was

God's desire, pleasure, and His choice to send His only begotten Son.

> For God so loved the world, that he gave his only begotten Son, that whosoever believeth in him should not perish, but have everlasting life. (John 3:16)

So we know it was God's will to send his only Son, and the Bible called Him the Word.

> In the beginning was the Word, and the Word was with God, and the Word was God. (John 1:1)

> And the Word was made flesh, and dwelt among us, (and we beheld his glory, the glory as of the only begotten of the Father) full of grace and truth. (John 1:14)

So the will of God and the Word of God are the same. In other words, if you have the Word of God you have the will of God. When I have God's Word on whatever I'm preparing to do, I have His will on it. Get the Word of God on it, and you have the will of God on it.

When you get the Word on it, you must have the Word of God that is rightly divided. You cannot pull scriptures out of their original context and make them fit an issue you may be having.

> Study to shew thyself approved unto God, a workman that needeth not to be ashamed, rightly dividing the word of truth. (2 Tim 2:15)

When you want to rightly divide the Word of God, answer these questions about the particular passage you are studying:

> Who is doing the talking?
> Who is the scripture talking to?
> What dispensation (period of time) is it talking within?

Let's "rightly divide" the following verse.

> But my God shall supply all your need according to his riches in glory by Christ Jesus. (Phil. 4:19)

Paul is talking to the Philippians who are under the Grace Dispensation—not the Law. Those under grace had sown into Paul's ministry when no one else had sown, and he says in this verse that "God will supply your needs because of how you supplied my needs." Paul is illustrating a principle of giving.

The Philippian Church was the smallest of all churches located in the Macedonian region. So, we can also learn from this verse that you don't have to be the largest church or the richest person to get the will of God in your life. We just need to give it all that we have in attending to the Word of God. God is a keeper of His Word (Num. 23:19).

EVERYTHING I NEED IS IN GOD'S WORD

> Jesus answered and said unto him, If a man love me, he will keep my words: and my Father will love him, and we will come unto him, and make our abode with him. (John 14:23)

Wherever the Lord is, there is everything you need. So when I have God's Word, I have whatever I need. God promised to keep His Word to man. As long as we have His Word and not some other word, we will have what the word says.

> So shall my word be that goeth forth out of my mouth: it shall not return unto me void, but it shall accomplish that which I please, and it shall prosper in the thing whereto I sent it. (Isa. 55:11)

The Word of God goes out and accomplishes what it was sent out to do and returns as accomplished and not void. God watches over His Word to perform it, and He does so through us—not from Heaven like a dictator. Many people believe God is sitting in heaven just waiting to fill some earthly order like a heavenly bellhop, but that is not the way it goes. We speak the Word of God through having assurance in His Word, trusting and relying on His Word and the finished work of Jesus to bring to pass what He said.

> Then said the Lord unto me, "Thou hast well seen: for I will hasten my word to perform it." (Jer. 1:12)

Jesus set the example for all mankind for all time when He used the Word to answer the temptation of Satan in the wilderness:

> And Jesus being full of the Holy Ghost returned from Jordan, and was led by the Spirit into the wilderness, Being forty days tempted of the devil. And in those days he did eat nothing: and when they were ended, he afterward hungered. And the devil said unto him, If thou be the Son of God, command this stone that it be made bread. And Jesus answered him, saying, It is written, That man shall not live by bread alone, but by every

word of God. And the devil, taking him up into an high mountain, shewed unto him all the kingdoms of the world in a moment of time. And the devil said unto him, All this power will I give thee, and the glory of them: for that is delivered unto me; and to whomsoever I will I give it. If thou therefore wilt worship me, all shall be thine. And Jesus answered and said unto him, Get thee behind me, Satan: for it is written, Thou shalt worship the Lord thy God, and him only shalt thou serve. And he brought him to Jerusalem, and set him on a pinnacle of the temple, and said unto him, If thou be the Son of God, cast thyself down from hence: For it is written, He shall give his angels charge over thee, to keep thee: And in their hands they shall bear thee up, lest at any time thou dash thy foot against a stone. And Jesus answering said unto him, It is said, Thou shalt not tempt the Lord thy God. And when the devil had ended all the temptation, he departed from him for a season. (Luke 4:1-13)

Jesus answered every issue with the Word of God, and we must do the same in our lives for every issue we face. Even the Devil had to leave Jesus for a season after being totally defeated by the Word of God. I don't know how long a season is or how long your season might be, but when you are in your season, nothing is missing, and nothing is broken. While you are in your season, allow the Word of God to minister to you as the angels did for Jesus, and be restored and refreshed.

THE WORD OF GOD HAS PROVEN WHAT THE WILL OF GOD IS

We are the ones who need to be proven in order for us to know who we are because the Word of God has already been proven. Many times, we assume we would respond to a certain situation in a certain way. But when pressure comes—and it will come— we do not always respond as we ought to. Hurricane Katrina was a natural event that tested the will and resolve of over a million people, and many were proven to be unprepared.

God's Word is proven from Genesis to Revelation. He delivered the children of Israel out of bondage on the exact day foretold in the prophecy.

> And it came to pass at the end of the four hundred and thirty years, even the selfsame day it came to pass, that all the hosts of the Lord went out from the land of Egypt. (Ex. 12:41)

Because that Abraham obeyed my voice, and kept my charge, my commandments, my statutes, and my laws. And Isaac dwelt in Gerar. (Gen. 26:5-6)

Then Isaac sowed in that land, and received in the same year an hundredfold: and the Lord blessed him. (Gen. 26:12)

Here are two places where you can establish in your heart that God's Word is already proven. Jesus said to the people of His time that if they destroyed "this temple", He would raise it again in three days. And the Word of God came to pass again, and with all power in His hand, Jesus finished the work at the cross. It is finished. We have the Word of God as proof.

When God raised Jesus from the dead, He proved His Word once and for all time. God does not need to prove Himself. We need to be proven to show where our hearts are for our own sakes. God already knows where our hearts are.

IF GOD SAID IT, HE WILL DO IT

I believe God, and if God said it, He will do it! The only problem with this statement for everyone is this question: "Did God really say it?" Too many times, people have quoted something or misquoted something said by God only to be disappointed and not see it come to pass... because God didn't say it in the first place. Even worse than God being misquoted is following some traditional family saying from some relative like "Big Momma" or "Big Papa." The issue is that whoever gave the word has to back up the word with results, and that is most likely not going to happen. Because man's traditions are limited and man's words are limited, we get limited results or no results in some cases. I don't know how you feel about it, but I want good success every time.

> This book of the law shall not depart out of thy mouth; but thou shalt meditate therein day and night, that thou mayest observe to do according to all that is written therein: for then thou shalt make thy way prosperous, and then thou shalt have good success. (Josh. 1:8)

God is a keeper of His Word, and He never fails to keep it. And His Word is proven.

Whenever you want to do anything in life, always start with the Word of God and prayer. Don't start and then find out later what He said. Start first with the Word.

> But seek ye first the kingdom of God, and his righteousness; and all these things shall be added unto you. (Matt. 6:33)

The Kingdom of God is simply the method of God. The Kingdom is how God accomplishes things. I use this analogy when explaining the Kingdom of God. Every king has a kingdom, and in that kingdom, there are rules to live by. When you follow the kingdom rules, you are extended all the rights the kingdom has to offer. You get to live inside the walls of the kingdom and under its protection and blessings. So long as you abide and live by the king's decrees, you prosper.

Likewise, we are in the Kingdom of God. He has laws, statues, decrees, and a covenant for us to live by, and so long as we abide under the covenant, we are blessed. Therefore, it is highly important to know what the covenant of God offers accurately and consistently in order to have full success in the blessing of God. A partial understanding is no understanding.

> Wisdom is the principal thing; therefore get wisdom: and with all thy getting get understanding. (Prov. 4:7)

The Word of God even goes further to say that, because men have used their own traditions, they have made what God said useless and ineffective.

Making the word of God of none effect through your tradition, which ye have delivered: and many such like things do ye. (Mark 7:13)

I want what God has for me, so I will get God's Word on whatever I attempt to do before I attempt to do it. I won't tell you how many times I have failed at doing what I thought I had God's Word on only to find out it was some other word or tradition handed down from someone. Vice versa, every time I had the Word of God on what I was doing, we had great success.

Preacher, how do you get God's Word on it? I'm glad you asked. Consider whatever you are doing through the lens of the Bible. Look in the Scripture for the Word on it.

TITHING

Honour the Lord with thy substance, and with the firstfruits of all thine increase: So shall thy barns be filled with plenty, and thy presses shall burst out with new wine. (Prov. 3:9)

GIVING

Give, and it shall be given unto you; good measure, pressed down, and shaken together, and running over, shall men give into your bosom. For with the same measure that ye mete withal it shall be measured to you again. (Luke 6:38)

But this I say, He which soweth sparingly shall reap also sparingly; and he which soweth bountifully shall reap also bountifully. Every man according as he purposeth in his heart, so let him give; not grudgingly, or of necessity: for God loveth a cheerful giver. (2 Cor. 9:6-7)

A faithful man shall abound with blessings: but he that maketh haste to be rich shall not be innocent. (Prov. 28:20)

FRIENDSHIP

A man that hath friends must shew himself friendly: and there is a friend that sticketh closer than a brother. (Prov. 18:24)

Greater love hath no man than this, that a man lay down his life for his friends. (John 15:13)

SUCCESS

> This book of the law shall not depart out of thy
> mouth; but thou shalt meditate therein day and
> night, that thou mayest observe to do according to
> all that is written therein: for then thou shalt
> make thy way prosperous, and then thou shalt
> have good success. (Josh. 1:8)

> But be ye doers of the word, and not hearers only,
> deceiving your own selves. (Jam. 1:22)

Whatever you are attempting to do, get the Word of God
on it first. Don't start anything without the Word of God and
prayer because, in order to pray effectively, you must have the
Word of God. Prayer is simply saying what God said and being
in agreement with what He said. This will ensure success because
you are saying and doing only what He said when He said it and
how He said it. Jesus said, "I only do what my Father says."

> Then said Jesus unto them, When ye have lifted
> up the Son of man, then shall ye know that I am
> he, and that I do nothing of myself; but as my
> Father hath taught me, I speak these things. And
> he that sent me is with me: the Father hath not

left me alone; for I do always those things that please him. (John 8:28-29)

The Will of God Is Not a Mystery

Have you heard this old saying: "Great is the mystery of God"? It means that God is keeping things a mystery from the saints. I believe they do not know what to say, and this is a cop out. For most of my early Christian life, I had heard people use this when they could not explain what the will of God was for their lives or for another person's life. I have found in the Word of God that it is simply not so. God is pleased to tell us what His will is for us. No, I do not believe that everything is explained in life. Some things will not be known or understood until we see Jesus in Heaven. However, the Bible is clear. In the following scriptures, God shows us that He wants us to know His will and gives it to us in the Word of God.

> And he said, Unto you it is given to know the mysteries of the kingdom of God: but to others in parables; that seeing they might not see, and hearing they might not understand. Unto to you is anyone who believes in Jesus for salvation, because God is no respecter of persons.
> (Luke 8:10)

Then Peter opened his mouth, and said, Of a truth I perceive that God is no respecter of persons. (Acts 10:34)

Even the mystery which hath been hid from ages and from generations, but now is made manifest to his saints: To whom God would make known what is the riches of the glory of this mystery among the Gentiles; which is Christ in you, the hope of glory. (Col. 1:26-27)

We are the saints of God because we believed in Jesus for our salvation.

Having made known unto us the mystery of his will, according to his good pleasure which he hath purposed in himself. (Eph. 1:9)

IT IS GOD'S GOOD PLEASURE TO LET US KNOW

If any of you lack wisdom, let him ask of God, that giveth to all men liberally, and upbraideth not; and it shall be given him. But let him ask in faith, nothing wavering. For he that wavereth is like a wave of the sea driven with the wind and tossed. For let not that man think that he shall receive any thing of the Lord. A double minded man is unstable in all his ways. (Jam. 1:5-8)

If any of us lack wisdom, God will give it to us. We find out the will of God by using our faith. Don't go by your feelings or emotions. Find the Word of God on it. The Word has something to say on everything we are facing. If you can't hear or understand what the Word is saying, find a good Bible-teaching ministry and get connected. Learn the Word of God, and ask questions from trustworthy men and women of God who are proven and authorized by the pastor.

HINDRANCES TO KNOWING GOD'S WILL

- Not being "Born Again"
- Not reading the Word of God
- Not mediating on the Word of God
- Listening to other people versus the Word of God
- Too many minds about the Word of God
- Taking scripture out of context or not "rightly dividing the Word of God"
- Not having received the Baptism of Holy Spirit

The last one is so important because Jesus said that He would not leave us in the world comfortless but that He would send another person, the Holy Spirit, who is just like Him. The Holy Spirit would come, and His job would be to show us things and teach us about things to help us while we are in this fallen world. Why would anyone not want help?

> If ye then, being evil, know how to give good gifts unto your children: how much more shall your heavenly Father give the Holy Spirit to them that ask him? (Luke 11:13)

Some people have not asked for a number of reasons, but the bottom line is this: If you do not ask, you will not receive. The Holy Spirit is critical for knowing the will of God. Can you make it without the Holy Spirit? Yes, but why would you want to go without heavenly help. If you have not been baptized in the Holy Spirit as the scripture says, then don't wait! Ask for the Baptism. There are only two requirements: your salvation and asking. Find a Spirit-filled, Bible-teaching church that will help you to understand and receive. The will of God is available to you. Knowing it is critical.

> For as many as are led by the Spirit of God, they are the sons of God. For ye have not received the

spirit of bondage again to fear; but ye have received the Spirit of adoption, whereby we cry, Abba, Father. (Rom. 8:14-15)

SONS AND DAUGHTERS HAVE RIGHTS THAT SERVANTS DO NOT

It was not the will of God to send a storm into the Gulf Coast, but God allowed it to happen. Storms come in off the coast all the time. We, however, have authority to speak against all things that are contrary to the Word of God, and that includes storms. We must, however, agree not to do things contrary to sound wisdom. New Orleans was willfully built below sea level, making it perilously open for disaster at any given time. I will leave it at that. God did not cause this disaster, nor did He send it. If we would have heeded all warnings and taken all of the necessary measures to avert calamity, we could have saved everyone. People were saying that the storm happened because of all the wickedness in New Orleans. If that's true, woe unto other cities much more perverse and wicked than New Orleans... even those not nearby water.

PUT THE WORD OF GOD IN YOUR EYES, MOUTH, AND EARS

To know the will of God, you must put the Word of God in your eyes by reading, studying, and meditating on that Word.

You must, then, put it in your heart by hearing it. As you speak the Word out loud, the first person to hear it will be you. You must put the Word of God in your mouth because...

> But what saith it? The word is nigh thee, even in thy mouth, and in thy heart: that is, the word of faith, which we preach; That if thou shalt confess with thy mouth the Lord Jesus, and shalt believe in thine heart that God hath raised him from the dead, thou shalt be saved. For with the heart man believeth unto righteousness; and with the mouth confession is made unto salvation.
> (Rom. 10:8-10)

It is not enough only to believe the Word of God; we must speak that Word with our mouths. Saying what the Word says in faith brings us into agreement with the promises that God has already made available. And it brings success.

This is not a formula to be repeated mindlessly. It is the truth that brings one success according to the Word of God. You don't have to know every scripture in the Bible to have God move on your behalf. Why? Because He already moved on your behalf when He sent Jesus to die for you. However, you must use God's Word and walk in agreement with that Word if you want God to be involved in your life.

Choose the Word of God to live by… not based on how you feel or what someone may have said to you. Keep choosing the Word until you see what you are looking for.

CHAPTER 6

RENEW YOUR MIND TO THE WILL OF GOD

We have been taught a lot of things that are not necessarily in the Bible. For most of our lives, we have been taught the world's system for living life, and a great majority of what we have been taught about life is not scriptural. For most of our early lives, we have been taught family traditions, cultural traditions, and secular traditions but not the Word of God. Because we have been taught so many ungodly ways and means of living, it seems natural and truthful. After all, so many people have said it. It's the idea that "perception is reality."

This is why an un-renewed mind cannot receive truth. That's right! An un-renewed mind cannot receive truth, and it will reject truth when error seems right in one's heart. Before the storm, people were getting truth about how bad the storm was going to be. Yet because of tradition and the coastal culture of storms, the information being communicated was downgraded to less than the truth.

Believers are the same. If their minds have not been renewed by the Word of God, they will override truth and follow tradition and culture.

Here is a good example of a secular saying I've heard: "A piece of man is better than no man." This is not found in the Word of God. Generally, older women have said this to younger women who are seeking companionship. It is their way of encouragement to at least get some kind of a man in one's life. In other words, where companionship is concerned, they should lower their standards and not use the Word of God.

Yet the Bible says, "Whoso findeth a wife findeth a good thing, and obtaineth favour of the Lord" (Prov. 18:22). A woman, first of all, should not be looking for a man. According to the Word of God, the man should be seeking after her.

Second, it is implying that the woman should be lost so she can be found… not lost or hiding in a cave, literally speaking, but lost in the things of God. The example I have used many times is found in the story of Rebecca.

> And before I had done speaking in mine heart, behold, Rebekah came forth with her pitcher on her shoulder; and she went down unto the well, and drew water: and I said unto her, Let me drink, I pray thee. And she made haste, and let down her pitcher from her shoulder, and said,

Drink, and I will give thy camels drink also: so I drank, and she made the camels drink also. (Gen. 24:45-46)

You can see in this true to life story that Rebekah was lost in the things of her father. She was not concerned with finding a husband. God, however, had another plan.

My revelation from this passage of scripture is that, when you are lost in the things of God and you are taking care of the Father's business, He will take care of your business. That's true even if He has to send someone to you from afar. Get lost in the ministry where you are doing the business of the Lord, and He will do business for you.

Knowing that whatsoever good thing any man doeth, the same shall he receive of the Lord, whether he be bond or free. (Eph. 6:8)

Get lost in helping someone else get what they are looking for, and you will receive the same.

People are afraid to get lost in doing for others because they think they are going to lose their place in line, so to speak. When it comes to serving and giving anything for the Kingdom's sake, you will never lose.

And he said unto them, Verily I say unto you, There is no man that hath left house, or parents, or brethren, or wife, or children, for the kingdom of God's sake, Who shall not receive manifold more in this present time, and in the world to come life everlasting. (Luke 18:29-30)

And Jesus answered and said, Verily I say unto you, There is no man that hath left house, or brethren, or sisters, or father, or mother, or wife, or children, or lands, for my sake, and the gospel's, But he shall receive an hundredfold now in this time, houses, and brethren, and sisters, and mothers, and children, and lands, with persecutions; and in the world to come eternal life. (Mark 10:29-30)

RENEWING YOUR MIND IS A LIFE-LONG PROCESS

As believers in God, we have been "born again" in spirit only... not in the mind nor in the body. So in order to get the mind straightened out, we must renew it according to the Word of God. That is a life-long process.

And be not conformed to this world: but be ye transformed by the renewing of your mind, that ye may prove what is that good, and acceptable, and perfect, will of God. (Rom. 12:2)

Don't become so well-adjusted to your culture that you fit into it without even thinking. Instead, fix your attention on God. You'll be changed from the inside out. Readily recognize what He wants from you, and quickly respond to it. Unlike the culture around you, always dragging you down to its level of immaturity, God brings the best out of you. He develops well-formed maturity in you.

> Do not be conformed to this world (this age), [fashioned after and adapted to its external, superficial customs], but be transformed (changed) by the [entire] renewal of your mind [by its new ideals and its new attitude], so that you may prove [for yourselves] what is the good and acceptable and perfect will of God, even the thing which is good and acceptable and perfect [in His sight for you]. (Rom. 12:2, AMP)

A good example of this is the conversation Jesus had with Nicodemus one night concerning being "born again."

The same came to Jesus by night, and said unto him, Rabbi, we know that thou art a teacher come from God: for no man can do these miracles that thou doest, except God be with him. Jesus answered and said unto him, Verily, verily, I say unto thee, Except a man be born again, he cannot see the kingdom of God. (John 3:2-3)

Jesus was speaking about the process of salvation to a man who had not renewed his mind to the New Covenant because that Covenant was not yet available. My point is that the man could not receive the truth because his mind was un-renewed. One can readily see what a hard time he was having. Nicodemus was very troubled by the salvation process until he asked Jesus how a man could go back into his mother's womb and be born again. Jesus was speaking about spiritual things to a man with an un-regenerated spirit and an un-renewed mind.

This also happened during the storm. People had not renewed their minds to the new systems for detecting and tracking storms. They thought it was business as usual and that they could do what they had always done. They would just ride out the storm.

Renewing your mind must be an act of your own will. In other words, you must want to renew your mind. The good thing about mind renewal is that God makes this process available to everyone.

I beseech you therefore, brethren, by the mercies of God, that ye present your bodies a living sacrifice, holy, acceptable unto God, which is your reasonable service. And be not conformed to this world: but be ye transformed by the renewing of your mind, that ye may prove what is that good, and acceptable, and perfect, will of God. (Rom. 12:1-2)

Getting a new mind as it pertains to life is not easy, but it is simple. We have learned so many things that are contrary to the Word of God. And they are embedded in our memories and physical lives. These obstacles are hard to overcome. But "thanks be unto God who gives us the victory," we can overcome all things with the Word of God. It's very simple. We renew our minds by exchanging what we think for what the Word of God says. We exchange our ways and ideas for God's ways and His ideas. As we said earlier, "Get the Word of God on it." We exchange our ways of thinking for God's way of thinking.

Finally, brethren, whatsoever things are true, whatsoever things are honest, whatsoever things are just, whatsoever things are pure, whatsoever things are lovely, whatsoever things are of good report; if there be any virtue, and if there be any praise, think on these things. Those things, which ye have both learned, and received, and heard, and seen in me, do: and the God of peace shall be with you. (Phil. 4:8-9)

TRANSFORMATION DOES NOT COME OVERNIGHT

Most people don't realize that their way of thinking did not happen overnight. It was a long process. Likewise, transformation doesn't take place overnight. You did not develop your mindset in a day, or a week, or a month, or even in one year. Therefore, don't be discouraged if it doesn't happen all at once. Change is not change until you change.

I know some people who have experienced divine renewal of the mind instantly, but those are the exceptions and not the rule. Renewal of the mind happens over a process of time. It begins when you accept the Word of God as truth by faith and then exchange that Word for what you think and believe. I cannot stress enough that it is impossible for an un-renewed mind to receive the Word.

So, before we go any further, begin the renewal process by inviting the Lord to be your Savior by grace through faith, and say, "I accept the Word of God as the final authority in my life." Now, knowing that the transformation of your mind is a process, let's start the process.

Begin to measure whatever you think is right against God's Word, and exchange what you think for what God says. Make God the final authority. Make Him the umpire of your life. Let the Word of God call the strikes like an umpire. Strike out all of the stuff like man's traditions, family traditions, secular humanism, and secular teaching. Throw out anything that isn't Bible-based.

Allow the Word to reign free in your life by reading and meditating on that Word and by exchanging it for your natural understanding of truth. You will find great success in all of your endeavors when God's Word is calling the plays. The Word of God is the umpire in your life. It's not what you think or feel or what someone else said but the Word of God. It may not change overnight, but you will begin to gain peace and good results quickly, and your life will change before you know it.

You should not take any shortcuts. Allow everything to process fully. All things must come as designed in order to get full benefit from them. Remember that the children of Israel wandered in the desert for 40 years because they did not follow the process. They murmured, suffered loss, became sick, and some died in the process.

The process is designed for you personally. It will get some things into you and some other things out of you.

Jacob is another good example. It was the process that revealed the trickster inside of him. As a result, his name was changed to Israel which meant he would "rule as God."

Do not abort the process! It will only be repeated until you get what God has intended for you to get out of it. What if Joseph had aborted the process for his life and missed being elevated to second-in-command in the court of Pharaoh? He and his family probably would not have made it. Remember it's not all about you; however, there is something in it for you.

Not following all the instructions in the process will only yield frustration and lengthen the time in the process. Partial obedience is no obedience.

For you, the process has been designed to do good and not bad. It has been designed to bring you to a good place and not to disaster.

> For I know the thoughts that I think toward you,
> saith the Lord, thoughts of peace, and not of evil,
> to give you an expected end. (Jer. 29:11)

Don't hate the process. That would be a distraction that would cause you to lose time and to be in a place longer than intended.

The process of God always leads to good results… not evil ones.

MAKE THE EXCHANGE

Change is difficult, but God makes change easy and light. So, make the exchange!

> Take my yoke upon you, and learn of me; for I am meek and lowly in heart: and ye shall find rest unto your souls. For my yoke is easy, and my burden is light. (Matt. 11:29-30)

I'm not saying that everything in life must be difficult. In fact, when things become troublesome, God can make them easy and light. How? By exchanging what we believe for what He says in His Word. He doesn't take away the challenge of change, but He makes it easy and light.

The more you exchange what you believe for the Word of God, the more you will succeed. Exchange your mind for the mind of Christ.

> Let this mind be in you, which was also in Christ Jesus: Who, being in the form of God, thought it not robbery to be equal with God: But made himself of no reputation, and took upon him the form of a servant, and was made in the likeness of men: And being found in fashion as a man, he

humbled himself, and became obedient unto death, even the death of the cross. (Phil. 2:5-8)

We must let His mind be in us. In other words, do not resist! What mind are we talking about? The mind of Christ... the mind that was obedient to the Word of God all the way to death. Jesus said so many times, "I don't do what I want to do but I do what my Father tells me to do and that only." That is the same mind every believer should have in this world. I no longer waste time telling the Devil "no!" I just say "yes!" to the Word of God in every situation.

Stop telling the Devil "no!" and tell God "yes!"

When I was growing up, it felt like my parents and other adults were saying "no!" to everything I wanted to do. Somebody even coined a phrase, "Just say 'no!' to drugs." How well did that work out? Just saying "no!" leaves a void, and that void will most likely be filled with a lust for the very thing to which you said "no!"

When the unclean spirit is gone out of a man, he walketh through dry places, seeking rest; and finding none, he saith, I will return unto my house whence I came out. And when he cometh, he findeth it swept and garnished. Then goeth he, and taketh to him seven other spirits more wicked than himself; and they enter in, and dwell there: and the last state of that man is worse than the first. (Luke 11:24-26)

Saying "no!" to the enemy may get him to leave, but he's coming back even stronger than before. So don't just say "no!" Go another step and exchange it for the Word of God. Put the Word of God in place and defeat the Enemy every time he shows up. Jesus used the Word and said "it is written" to defeat the Enemy every time. And the very same Word that Jesus had at His disposal, we have at ours.

And Jesus answered him, saying, It is written, That man shall not live by bread alone, but by every word of God. (Luke 4:4)

Listen to this! We have the same right and authority to use the Word of God on Earth as Jesus did. Jesus may be in Heaven, but we and His Word are still here on Earth.

Herein is our love made perfect, that we may have boldness in the day of judgment: because as he is, so are we in this world. (1 John 4:17)

WALKING IN AGREEMENT WITH THE WORD

Jesus used the Word of God against every test of the Enemy, but for the Word to have success, Jesus had to be in agreement with it.

> Can two walk together, except they be agreed? (Amos 3:3)

This scripture is talking about being in agreement with God... not just "walking together." In other words, God is under no obligation to work with us or to help us accomplish anything if what we are doing is not in agreement with what He has said in His Word.

In order to get the benefits of storm relief or disaster relief, people had to be in agreement with the plan to obtain relief. If they did not comply with the plan for relief, they would not get assistance. Sounds hard, but it was true.

Many believers are living frustrated lives because they are looking for something that is not coming because they did not know how to be in agreement with the Word of God. Doing what you feel or think is right does not put you in agreement with the God's Word. You don't have to like it, but you must agree and walk in it for it to cause you to prosper.

Don't waste time in disagreement. It's another trap of the Enemy to keep you from having what God promised. Once again, being in disagreement is a trap of Satan to keep you from finding areas where you do agree and then working on those areas in which you are out of agreement.

The Enemy knows he cannot stop you from having what has been promised by God. However, if he can get you into disagreement with God, you will stop your own progress. When you agree to anything the Devil is offering, you will lose your identity and begin to live in shame.

> How should one chase a thousand, and two put
> ten thousand to flight, except their Rock had sold
> them, and the Lord had shut them up?
> (Deut. 32:30)

In other words, be sold out to the Word of God no matter what anyone else says.

I'm still in the process of transforming my own mind because, every time I read the Bible, I receive fresh revelation from the Lord. We will be in this transformative state until we receive our glorified bodies in Heaven. On Earth, our spirit man is the only one that is born again, regenerated, complete, and whole.

For we know that if our earthly house of this tabernacle were dissolved, we have a building of God, an house not made with hands, eternal in the heavens For in this we groan, earnestly desiring to be clothed upon with our house which is from heaven: If so be that being clothed we shall not be found naked. For we that are in this tabernacle do groan, being burdened: not for that we would be unclothed, but clothed upon, that mortality might be swallowed up of life. (2 Cor. 5:1-4)

Until we receive our glorified bodies in Heaven, we are renewing our minds daily. The process of renewing the mind is a life-long journey and not a one-time event.

During the Hurricane Katrina storm evacuation, I saw people in agreement like never before. Usually, when a major storm rolls in from the Gulf of Mexico, people who live on the coast tend to attempt to ride it out and batten down the hatches. This time, it was not the same old coastal mentality of wait and see. People actually began to walk in agreement by obeying the instructions of those in charge and evacuating sooner than later.

One example of a person who renewed his mind was the Apostle Paul, formerly known as Saul. Paul began to change on the road to Damascus. After being blinded by the light of the

Lord, three days later, he received his sight. Thus began the renewal of his mind.

Barnabas, a disciple of Christ guided, Paul's process of renewal. Barnabas tutored Paul for over 15 years before they separated. The Apostle Paul went off on his own to preach the gospel to the Gentiles.

> Then fourteen years after I went up again to Jerusalem with Barnabas, and took Titus with me also. (Gal. 2:1)

Paul did not abort the process or take any shortcuts. He remained faithful to Barnabas until he had fulfilled his calling in Christ. Many people today, even ministers, have not been tutored by another minister of the gospel. They simply "get called," get a license to preach, and start a ministry. I believe that's why there are so many failures in our churches, both in the pulpit and in the pews.

Many Christians and church members are submitted to these pastoral ministries and, thus, live defeated lives. They are saved but not living as victorious Christians. They are simply not getting the Bible's promised results in their lives because of preachers who have cut short the process of God by not giving them rightly-divided, Biblical truth.

Paul renewed his mind to the gospel of Christ Jesus, and Barnabas helped him. He only taught what he had been taught by the Holy Spirit. It was the gospel of Jesus Christ... not Paul's gospel. Not John's gospel. But the gospel of Jesus Christ.

> But by the grace of God I am what I am: and his grace which was bestowed upon me was not in vain; but I laboured more abundantly than they all: yet not I, but the grace of God which was with me. (1 Cor. 15:10)

> Paul, called to be an apostle of Jesus Christ through the will of God, and Sosthenes our brother. (1 Cor. 1:1)

Instead of remaining the Saul who persecuted Christians, he became the Apostle of Jesus who led people to his Lord. This process happened after years of being faithful to Barnabas and to the Word of God.

There was nothing pleasant about the evacuation of those people who had survived Katrina. However, upon completion of that process and after relief had been obtained, it was shouting time, and all the bad memories were washed away.

Paul renewed his mind so much so that he no longer remembered who that first guy (Saul) was. Paul wrote the recipe for believers to renew their minds by saying,

> Brethren, I count not myself to have apprehended: but this one thing I do, forgetting those things which are behind, and reaching forth unto those things which are before, I press toward the mark for the prize of the high calling of God in Christ Jesus. (Phil. 3:13-14)

For the Apostle Paul, renewing his mind was the key to having great success in ministry and life.

Get a real relationship with Jesus, and begin the process of renewing your mind with the Word of God as it pertains to everything you think and believe.

God will not put you in ministry if you have not been faithful in another man's ministry, and you don't get to say when you have been faithful. Someone else has to call you faithful.

> And if ye have not been faithful in that which is another man's, who shall give you that which is your own. (Luke 16:12)

Learn how to forget the past and look toward to the future. You cannot go forward while looking backward. Your future is the antidote where the past is concerned.

Remember it is not you but Christ in you who is your hope for glory. It is He who facilitates the transformation and renewal.

> To whom God would make known what is the riches of the glory of this mystery among the Gentiles; which is Christ in you, the hope of glory Whom we preach, warning every man, and teaching every man in all wisdom; that we may present every man perfect in Christ Jesus: Whereunto I also labour, striving according to his working, which worketh in me mightily.
> (Col. 1:27-29)

Take the Word of God, and make it the final authority for your life and ministry.

CHAPTER 7

THIS ONE THING

This last chapter was written solely to encourage storm survivors to look toward the future. And the way to look to the future is to focus on one thing at a time.

> Brethren, I count not myself to have apprehended: but this one thing I do, forgetting those things which are behind, and reaching forth unto those things which are before, I press toward the mark for the prize of the high calling of God in Christ Jesus. Let us therefore, as many as be perfect, be thus minded: and if in anything ye be otherwise minded, God shall reveal even this unto you. (Phil. 3:13-15)

Paul did it by not counting himself to have learned it all or known it all, but he chose to look forward and not behind... to the future and not to the past.

It's difficult to do many things at once. Even living in this generation, people are being told that, to make it, you must be able to multitask. This is just another example of how the secular society has sold the idea that multitasking is the way to go for everything. However, I'm still of the school of thought that teaches, "Be the greatest at one thing at a time, and you will be very successful."

The Ford Motor Company was the best at the assembly line process in building automobiles. Now, they are in the fourth generation of family building automobiles and wealth. I could go on listing many people who have achieved great success by being the best at one thing.

During my high school years, I chose not to participate in several extracurricular activities in order to concentrate on one thing; that was being a drummer. In just one year's time, I went from unknown to the lead drum major of the band and the number one drummer on the drum line. I focused on one thing for a whole year. And that one thing was how to play the trap set. By doing so, I was rewarded with the coveted spot in the jazz band. I was granted this honor even ahead of the senior drummer.

So we encouraged the storm survivors to put their focus on what was in front of them… one thing at a time.

Another analogy often used in the secular world is this: "How do you eat an elephant? One bite at a time."

His lord said unto him, well done, thou good and faithful servant: thou hast been faithful over a few things, I will make thee ruler over many things: enter thou into the joy of thy lord. (Matt. 25:21)

Even the Bible teaches multitasking but only with a few things at one time. God will then cause the faithful to be rulers over much.

So many times, people have been told to do what the Word says and promised they will be successful as a result. And they are right. However, it's overwhelming to think you must do all of these things to make it. There are so many scriptures available for instruction. A person can become distressed trying to see which one is for them at a given time. That is why I believe I received "This One Thing" teaching... to help people see that they don't have to know the whole Bible to get through transitions in life.

REMEMBERING IS AUTOMATIC; FORGETTING TAKES EFFORT

When you're in a catastrophic event like Hurricane Katrina, it's hard to forget the past and move on toward the future because remembering is so easy. Forgetting takes effort. You have heard it said, "Just forget about it and move on!" Well, that's easy for others to say but hard for you to do. Why? Because of the memories.

God designed us with the ability to remember by gifting us with memory capacity. I'm not asking that people not remember, but I am asking them not to camp out in memories. We can use good memories of past success to give us momentum to go forward, but we should not camp out in them. Even good memories ought not to dominate our thought lives.

Living in past successes can also be just as detrimental as dwelling on past failures. The past should not be used to self-medicate but rather as a catalyst for forward momentum. Good or bad, we ought not to camp out on life's past successes or failures. Why? Because we'd end up marching in place with no forward action.

It's normal to have memories, but don't let your memories have you.

Forgetting takes effort. For example, think about when you loan someone money, and they purposely go out of their way not to see you. If they don't see you, they can avoid the responsibility of debt repayment. Or so they think. Much effort is being used to avoid facing the obligation to pay you back. Some people will see you in the marketplace and take the other aisle to keep from being reminded.

When the children of Israel left captivity, they had memories of the past. As soon as they came upon hard times, they chose to remember the past, even saying that they had it better in Egypt under captivity than being free in the wilderness.

> We remember the fish, which we did eat in Egypt freely; the cucumbers, and the melons, and the leeks, and the onions, and the garlic: But our soul is dried away: there is nothing at all, beside this manna, before our eyes. (Num. 11:5-6)

They forgot that, in Egypt, they had been slaves. Selective amnesia can be a very dangerous thought process. It wasn't as good in Egypt as they recalled it had been. What makes it even more astounding is that they were eating manna from Heaven every day. It was "Angel's food", and they did not see the blessing in it.

Some transitions are blessings in disguise. They provide opportunities to hit the "reset button" on life. They are opportunities to see God make all things work together for our good.

The ability to remember has been given to us by God not so we can relive the past and go into a spiral of depression but to recall the many goodnesses of the Lord and how He has brought us out of trouble with His mighty, outstretched hand. He has caused us to prosper and thereby taught us how we should love people as He has loved us.

This One Thing: God Has Never Failed

This one thing we ought always to remember: God has never failed us. There is not one thing He has promised that He has failed to deliver.

> And, behold, this day I am going the way of all the earth: and ye know in all your hearts and in all your souls, that not one thing hath failed of all the good things which the Lord your God spake concerning you; all are come to pass unto you, and not one thing hath failed thereof. (Josh. 23:14)

> God is not a man, that he should lie; neither the son of man, that he should repent: hath he said, and shall he not do it? or hath he spoken, and shall he not make it good? (Num. 23:19)

Throughout the Bible, God has never failed to do what He said He would do.

The issue is that we should always ask whether or not what we are trying to do is God-directed. Sometimes, people are looking for things to happen that simply do not have God's

Word of authorization. But because they "need" it, they think it should just happen without them asking. God does know our every need, but He has established a relationship with us as Father and said for us to ask Him for whatever we need and that He would supply that need. So then, the prescribed method of acquiring what is available is to ask for what we need.

These are some scriptures concerning how we should be asking to get our needs met.

> We will rejoice in thy salvation, and in the name of our God we will set up our banners: the Lord fulfil all thy petitions. (Psa. 20:5)

> And this is the confidence that we have in him, that, if we ask any thing according to his will, he heareth us: And if we know that he hear us, whatsoever we ask, we know that we have the petitions that we desired of him. (1 John 5:14-15)

> Be careful for nothing; but in everything by prayer and supplication with thanksgiving let your requests be made known unto God. (Phil. 4:6)

As discussed earlier, whatever you are about to do in life, get God's Word first, and you will then have His will. Start with prayer. Don't let it be an afterthought. Ask the Father, and He will answer. One thing with which I have found great success is this: after praying, simply wait for an answer. Do not keep talking. Rather, say, "Speak, Lord, and your servant will hear." Then, wait for it. Be still, and in a still, small voice, the Lord will answer.

> And after the earthquake a fire; but the Lord was
> not in the fire: and after the fire a still small voice.
> (1 Kings 19:12)

The Holy Spirit is a gentleman in every respect. He does not come screaming and yelling out the instructions. No big hand is going to reach down from Heaven and grab you by the back of your neck and stop you from choosing the wrong thing. But thanks be unto God, our Father, who gives to us the victory in all things. If we choose incorrectly, He is able to cause things to work together in our favor. Knowing this, I feel that I can't make a bad decision in God.

> And we know that all things work together for
> good to them that love God, to them who are the
> called according to his purpose. (Rom. 8:28)

This means that some good things and some bad things are going to happen in this life. You are probably asking the same question I did some years ago: Why does God allow bad things to happen even to good people?

We live in a fallen world, and bad things happen in a fallen world. Go back to the beginning when Adam and Eve fell from grace. Their world and ours changed.

God did not fix the sin-broken world. He didn't immediately make it perfect once again. Rather, He sent a perfect sacrifice into the world, His only begotten Son, Jesus. He fulfilled the promise He had made to Adam and the Covenant He originally had cut with Abraham.

If God were to intervene in the world by correcting all the bad things that happen, He would no longer be God. He would become a dictator and not the Creator. God created us with free will and the ability to choose. So we need to choose life and not the things that cause death.

> I call heaven and earth to record this day against you, that I have set before you life and death, blessing and cursing: therefore choose life, that both thou and thy seed may live: That thou mayest love the Lord thy God, and that thou mayest obey his voice, and that thou mayest cleave unto him: for he is thy life, and the length of thy

days: that thou mayest dwell in the land which the Lord sware unto thy fathers, to Abraham, to Isaac, and to Jacob, to give them.
(Deut. 30:19-20)

We live in a fallen world, but we are a redeemed people. As such, we can overcome everything this fallen world brings against us.

Another reason why bad things happen to good people in this lost and dying world is that believers lack knowledge.

My people are destroyed for lack of knowledge: because thou hast rejected knowledge, I will also reject thee, that thou shalt be no priest to me: seeing thou hast forgotten the law of thy God, I will also forget thy children. (Hos. 4:6)

God's Word gives to us knowledge as to what has been made available to us by way of protection, authority, grace, mercy, and identity. The blood of Jesus is our protection as we remain under its covering. His precious blood protects the believer from the curse of sin. But, if we choose to say or do things in contradiction to the Word of God, we are opening ourselves to the forces of the Enemy.

> And they overcame him by the blood of the
> Lamb, and by the word of their testimony; and
> they loved not their lives unto the death.
> (Rev. 12:11)

We have authority over the Enemy today because Jesus has restored it to us. Adam gave it up in the Garden. Jesus won it back on Calvary.

As recorded in the Gospels, Satan attempted to give power and glory to Jesus. All the Son of God had to do was worship the Devil. I once thought, "How could he possibly tempt Jesus with power he does not possess?" Since then, I have found myself to have been in error. Our enemy did, in fact, possess such power.

> And the devil said unto him, All this power will I
> give thee, and the glory of them: for that is
> delivered unto me; and to whomsoever I will I
> give it. (Luke 4:6)

Adam gave away his authority and power when he chose to eat of the fruit of the Tree of the Knowledge of Good and Evil. But praise be unto God that He gave Jesus to us to take our place on the cross. It was there that He purchased the power back for us.

Jesus knowing that the Father had given all things into his hands, and that he was come from God, and went to God. (John 13:3)

Jesus has given to us the keys to the Kingdom of God, and we have power over the enemy today.

And I will give unto thee the keys of the kingdom of heaven: and whatsoever thou shalt bind on earth shall be bound in heaven: and whatsoever thou shalt loose on earth shall be loosed in heaven. (Matt. 16:19)

The enemy, Satan, is still trying to steal, kill, and destroy the people of God.

The thief cometh not, but for to steal, and to kill, and to destroy: I am come that they might have life, and that they might have it more abundantly. (John 10:8-10)

Satan knows that he cannot harm believers in his own power, so he lies in wait to steal the Word of God from our hearts. In that way, he can stop us from believing the promises of God that keep us safe from the evil one. After Satan steals the

Word, he then goes about killing and destroying the believer with ungodly thoughts that ultimately lead to destruction.

I have heard it said in times past that you cannot stop a bird from flying over your head, but you can stop him from building a nest in your hair. The same is true with ungodly thoughts from Satan. You can't stop thoughts from coming, but you can surely keep them from setting up a nest in your thinking. Do not allow thoughts to have power over you. Refuse to allow them to hang around. Reject ungodly thoughts, and cast them down. Replace them with what the Word of God says. Say this when an ungodly thought comes your way: "I don't receive this thought! I reject all such negative thinking, and I cast down every evil plan or imagination and replace it with the plan of God for my life."

THIS ONE THING: DESIRE TO SEEK AFTER THE LORD

You must have a desire to seek after the wisdom of God when making any transition in life.

> One thing have I desired of the Lord, that will I
> seek after; that I may dwell in the house of the
> Lord all the days of my life, to behold the beauty
> of the Lord, and to inquire in his temple.
> (Psa. 27:4)

"One thing" is what the Psalmist desires. He did not desire so many things that he lost track of what he was seeking.

This is a call to develop your relationship with the Lord by seeking Him in the temple and by coming together in fellowship. Yes, I'm getting ready to say what you think I'm going to say. You must seek regular fellowship in a local church. This is because one will have little or no confidence in asking the Father for anything without having regular fellowship and relationship with Him in worship.

Fellowship stengthens the bond between you, God, and the people in your community. Where there is no fellowship, there can be no confidence. Where there is no confidence, there is no asking. Not going to church does not make God angry with us, but it will cause our relationship to be hindered. God loves His children no matter what.

Have you ever had a great relationship with someone with whom you hardly ever spoke? What if you rarely spent any time with that person? That relationship probably did not last. Or, at best, it was weak. In order to have a great relationship, you must take time to fellowship.

I use this analogy occasionaly. I use If you had a girlfriend, and you only went to see her once every six months, you probably would not have kept that girlfriend for very long. You'll never get to know someone if you don't spend time with them.

God is our Father, and He is so good to us. No matter how we may miss the mark, we are still His children, and He loves us. As God's children, we must remember that our relationship with the Lord is strengthened when we have regular fellowship and communication. That means time in prayer and Bible study.

> Not forsaking the assembling of ourselves together, as the manner of some is; but exhorting one another: and so much the more, as ye see the day approaching. (Heb. 10:25)

> In the name of our Lord Jesus Christ, when ye are gathered together, and my spirit, with the power of our Lord Jesus Christ. (1 Cor. 5:4)

THIS ONE THING: BEING LAW-MINDED WILL CAUSE LACK

Being Law-minded will cause lack in our lives. In the story of the Rich Young Ruler, he thought he had done everything he needed to do in order to receive from Jesus, but he did not realize he was woefully lacking. He was trying to keep the same Law the Pharisees could not keep. Everytime you use the Law, you will come up lacking. Why? Because the Law was not designed to meet needs. It was designed to show how much we lack and just how badly we need the Savior, Jesus Christ.

> Then Jesus beholding him loved him, and said unto him, One thing thou lackest: go thy way, sell whatsoever thou hast, and give to the poor, and thou shalt have treasure in heaven: and come, take up the cross, and follow me. (Mark 10:21)

Don't get it twisted. Our minds should be on following the laws of the land, but "first seek ye the kingdom of God and all these things shall be added." In other words, we should not be so legalistic in our thinking that we forget just how much we need God.

We saw a lot of people come into the church during and shortly after the storm. A few weeks later, people began to fall back into the normal patterns of life and forgetting to fellowship. Choose not to wait for a storm to blow through your life or for some tragedy to strike. Be reminded all of the time that the Lord is the source of all your help at all times. Not just in troubled times.

> I will lift up mine eyes unto the hills, from whence cometh my help. My help cometh from the Lord, which made heaven and earth. He will

not suffer thy foot to be moved: he that keepeth thee will not slumber. Behold, he that keepeth Israel shall neither slumber nor sleep. The Lord is thy keeper: the Lord is thy shade upon thy right hand. The sun shall not smite thee by day, nor the moon by night. The Lord shall preserve thee from all evil: he shall preserve thy soul. The Lord shall preserve thy going out and thy coming in from this time forth, and even for evermore. (Psa. 121)

THIS ONE THING: ALWAYS CHOOSE THE BETTER PART

Mary chose the better part when Jesus was visiting in her home one day. However, she was criticized by her own sister. During times of transition, you may get criticized for accepting aid from certain sources. But where provisions are made to assist you, accept that help from the hand of God.

> But one thing is needful: and Mary hath chosen that good part, which shall not be taken away from her. (Luke 10:42)

You will need to hear the Word of God no matter where you are or in what circumstances you may find yourself. Martha got caught up in everything that was needed to make Jesus' visit an excellent one, but she forgot the "better part." The Lord was there to share the Word—instructions, revelations, something good for their soul.

In every transition, don't forget about the better part, which is the Word of God.

There was a time when I was in transition to another state and city. I waited far too long to find a ministry with which to connect. I began to feel disconnected and discombobuliated in my everyday life, and I knew right away that I had forgotten the "better part."

I found a ministry quickly. And soon, after getting connected, I got back on track. I was hearing God's Word, and things were better in all areas of my life.

THIS ONE THING: GOD CHOOSES TO FORGET OUR SINS

God chooses to forget our sins and iniquities.

> But this shall be the covenant that I will make with the house of Israel; After those days, saith the Lord, I will put my law in their inward parts, and write it in their hearts; and will be their God, and they shall be my people. And they shall teach no more every man his neighbor, and every man

his brother, saying, Know the Lord: for they shall all know me, from the least of them unto the greatest of them, saith the Lord; for I will forgive their iniquity, and I will remember their sin no more. (Jer. 31:33-34)

We need to understand that we have all sinned because we have all missed the mark and will miss the mark again in life. Because we live in a fallen world, the opportunity to miss is always present. But thanks be unto the Father that He does not hold anything against us because of His grace. The grace of God is on our lives because we have accepted Jesus as our personal Lord and Savior. Grace is His unmerited favor, which means that we did not earn it, nor did we have to work for it. But God has extended it to us by sending His only Son as the perfect sacrifice. He took our punishment for sins on Himself.

How do you know God has chosen to forget and not see our sin?

But God commendeth his love toward us, in that, while we were yet sinners, Christ died for us. (Rom. 5:8)

God knew we could not keep the Law, so He sent his Son to fulfill all of the Law for mankind. Now by grace through faith, we have been redeemed from the curse of the Law. Because we have been redeemed by God, Who sent His Son to die in our place, He would not waste His Son's precious blood just to turn around and call us sinners, condemn us, and keep bringing up our faults. No! When He sees the blood of Jesus, He does not see you or your mistakes.

And they overcame him by the blood of the Lamb, and by the word of their testimony; and they loved not their lives unto the death. (Rev. 12:11)

There is therefore now no condemnation to them which are in Christ Jesus, who walk not after the flesh, but after the Spirit. (Rom. 8:1)

As far as the east is from the west, so far hath he removed our transgressions from us. (Psa. 103:12)

I, even I, am he that blotteth out thy transgressions for mine own sake, and will not remember thy sins. (Isa. 43:25)

What I'm saying is that you are forgiven. God chose to forgive us, and He did it once and forever by sending His Son as the perfect sacrifice.

> Christ hath redeemed us from the curse of the law, being made a curse for us: for it is written, Cursed is every one that hangeth on a tree: That the blessing of Abraham might come on the Gentiles through Jesus Christ; that we might receive the promise of the Spirit through faith. (Gal. 3:13-14)

Because we are blessed by God, every transition in our lives leads to a blessing. Don't let anything or anyone move you from the place of faith in God. Never listen to anyone who says that you are not forgiven. Amen!

While God has forgiven us—for past, present, and future sins—we do not have a blank check to continue to live in sin, nor do we escape the consequences of sin in this life. Sin won't stop God's love, and neither will it undo your salvation. But there are consequences of sin.

If one man caused sin to come into the world, then one man's righteousness paid for it all.

> For if by one man's offence death reigned by one;
> much more they which receive abundance of grace
> and of the gift of righteousness shall reign in life
> by one, Jesus Christ. Therefore as by the offence
> of one judgment came upon all men to
> condemnation; even so by the righteousness of
> one the free gift came upon all men unto
> justification of life. For as by one man's
> disobedience many were made sinners, so by the
> obedience of one shall many be made righteous.
> (Rom. 5:17-19)

We are made righteous because of Jesus, but Jesus said to all those to whom He ministered, "Go and sin no more." But if you do sin, "you have an advocate" in Jesus forever. Your Savior will argue your case before the Judge of Heaven and Earth, His Father and yours.

> My little children, these things write I unto you,
> that ye sin not. And if any man sin, we have an
> advocate with the Father, Jesus Christ the
> righteous: And he is the propitiation for our sins:
> and not for ours only, but also for the sins of the
> whole world. (1 John 2:1-2)

Forget about the past, and look to your future in God.

> For I know the thoughts that I think toward you,
> saith the Lord, thoughts of peace, and not of evil,
> to give you an expected end. (Jer. 29:11)

The way to forget the past is to look to the future. You cannot drive a car going forward by looking in the rearview mirror. The more you concentrate on looking forward, the more you will go forward and not give the past undue thought.

Most people I know have a hard time forgetting the bad in their past. The way to forget is simple but not easy. Work hard at living in the present and looking toward the future so that there is no time for the past. Let the past be the past. Your part in this scenario is exactly that! Let it be… past!

> Let this mind be in you, which was also in Christ
> Jesus: Who, being in the form of God, thought it
> not robbery to be equal with God: But made
> himself of no reputation, and took upon him the
> form of a servant, and was made in the likeness of
> men: And being found in fashion as a man, he
> humbled himself, and became obedient unto
> death, even the death of the cross. (Phil. 2:5-8)

Let not your heart be troubled: ye believe in God,

believe also in me. (John 14:1)

The scriptures plainly say, "let this mind be in you" and "let not your heart be troubled." Your part in all of this is to not "let" it be so. In order to "let", you must allow the Word of God to be the final authority and choose not to let your emotions dictate your direction. Too many people let their emotions dictate the direction of their lives. When this happens, emotions can go in the wrong direction.

Emotions were designed by God, and they are perfect. However, emotions were never designed to lead us or control us. Emotions are designed to indicate something needs to be done. If your gas tank's "low-level light" comes on, it is indicating that the car is in need of fuel. You decide to get fuel. Getting mad at the car will not address the issue of low fuel.

This message was not an easy one for me, personally. Why? My mother lived with us for three weeks during the evacuation. She was very concerned about the house in which we grew up. She began to think it had been destroyed. She would not be able to return to the home she once knew.

When the city allowed people to return to the hurricane-stricken area, my mother and I found that the house was intact. Our surprise was surpassed only by the joy we felt.

It was a miracle! The houses in every direction from her home had been destroyed or damaged so extensively that they were all rendered totally uninhabitable. On all sides! Power had been restored, and Mom was able to return the very same day.

> For I know the thoughts that I think toward you,
> saith the Lord, thoughts of peace, and not of evil,
> to give you an expected end. (Jer. 29:11)

God has already considered what He has laid out for us. It's all good. We must, of course, walk out the Word by faith. But we know the fight is fixed. In Christ, we win!

> And he said, Hearken ye, all Judah, and ye inhabitants of Jerusalem, and thou king Jehoshaphat, Thus saith the Lord unto you, Be not afraid nor dismayed by reason of this great multitude; for the battle is not yours, but God's. (2 Chron. 20:15)

Transition is the moving of people or things from one place to another. You can move willingly or be moved by force. After making seven major transitions in my life, I prefer the "willingly" option. It is much to be preferred over and above being forced, coerced, or tricked into moving. Even if you don't remember anything else from this book, remember this one thing: God loves you, and God's love is what makes the difference. Looking to the future is the antidote for being stuck in the past.

We can have plans that may look like they are well thought out, on target, and linked in every way possible, but God has another plan. And it is all good!

39 NUGGETS TO REMEMBER FOR YOUR TRANSITION

1. Being "led by the Spirit" is not some spooky feeling or out-of-control, paranormal, or individual act. God has given to us His inspired Word to lead us throughout life. We must accept it as our final authority.

> For as many as are led by the Spirit of God, they are the sons of God. (Rom. 8:14)

2. When we don't know who or what is leading us, we could end up at the wrong destination. We might be forced to remain in the wrong place far longer than we intended to stay!

> And Jesus being full of the Holy Ghost returned from Jordan, and was led by the Spirit into the wilderness. (Luke 4:1)

3. The act of murmuring gives access to unwanted and unnecessary issues in life. Therefore, shut the door, and keep the Devil in the dark.

> Neither give place to the devil. (Eph. 4:27)

> It is the spirit that quickeneth; the flesh profiteth nothing: the words that I speak unto you, they are spirit, and they are life. (John 6:63)

4. God always has another plan for whatever you are facing. He will not stop loving you. Neither will He forsake you nor leave you alone.

> And he said, Hearken ye, all Judah, and ye inhabitants of Jerusalem, and thou king Jehoshaphat, Thus saith the Lord unto you, Be not afraid nor dismayed by reason of this great multitude; for the battle is not yours, but God's. (2 Chron. 20:15)

5. Choose not to develop your plan first! Ask God what His will is for your life.

6. People walking in different directions will never get to their desired and common destination.

7. Accept what God allows.

8. Whatever you are attempting to do, remember to hear the Word of God on it first. When you start with God's Word, success will not be far away.

9. Where there is the will of God, there is the way of God!

> And such as do wickedly against the covenant shall he corrupt by flatteries: but the people that do know their God shall be strong, and do exploits. (Dan. 11:32)

10. Knowing the will of God is always followed by instructions from the Word of God.

11. When a person wants you to know their will, they will communicate words that express complete instruction as to their desires. They will also let you know how you can benefit from following those instructions.

12. If you ever find yourself having to make a transition, please follow all the instructions accurately.

13. God's process always leads to good results and not evil ones.

For I know the thoughts that I think toward you, saith the Lord, thoughts of peace, and not of evil, to give you an expected end. (Jer. 29:11)

14. Renewing your mind to the Word of God is a life-long process, so stay in that process. There are no shortcuts, back doors, or windows of escape.

Nevertheless, not my will, but your will be done...

Abraham tried another process; Jacob tried another process; Peter...

15. An un-renewed mind cannot and will not accept the truth.

Jesus answered, Verily, verily, I say unto thee, Except a man be born of water and of the Spirit, he cannot enter into the kingdom of God. That which is born of the flesh is flesh; and that which is born of the Spirit is spirit. (John 3:5-6)

The Kingdom of God can be defined simply as God's way of doing things. It's just as kings would do in their own domain.

Because the carnal mind is enmity against God: for it is not subject to the law of God, neither indeed can be. (Rom. 8:7)

16. God will not communicate with you in your mind but with your spirit.

The spirit of man is the candle of the Lord, searching all the inward parts of the belly. (Prov. 20:27)

Dr. R.V. Layton, my pastor, says it like this: "The spirit of man is the flashlight of the Lord."

Your spirit talks to your mind, and some people think they are talking to themselves when this happens. I say you are talking to yourself because your spirit is the real you, and it sounds just like you.

17. When you are down and out, self-talk can be an encouragement to you but only if you use words of faith, positive confessions, and the promises of God.

> And David was greatly distressed; for the people spake of stoning him, because the soul of all the people was grieved, every man for his sons and for his daughters: but David encouraged himself in the Lord his God. (1 Sam. 30:6)

18. Do not abort the process. It will only be repeated until you get what God has intended for you to get out of it.

19. Some classes in life are worth repeating, but I do not recommend becoming a career student.

> Ever learning, and never able to come to the knowledge of the truth. (2 Tim. 3:7)

20. Don't hate the process because hating the process is a distraction that causes you to lose time and shortens the runway for life's takeoffs.

21. The more you exchange the Word of God for what you believe, the more you will succeed.

22. Learn how to forget the past and look toward the future.

23. You cannot go forward by looking backward.

24. Your future is the antidote for forgetting.

25. Remind yourself every day that it's not you doing the work but that it is Christ in you Who never runs out of supply.

26. Remember that, in this world of multitasking, one thing at a time can be liberating.

> Set yourself free by zeroing in on one thing at a time until that one thing is complete. Put the shotgun down.

27. Memory comes automatically. Forgetting takes effort.

28. Living on past successes can become detrimental if used to self-medicate and not as a catalyst for forward action.

29. You do not have to explain everything. We live in a fallen world where bad things happen to good people.

> You are living "in" this world, but you are not "of" this world. You have the spirit of Christ in you, and your address has changed.

> Pray that Heaven's way comes to the world.

30. We can have plans that may look like they are well thought out, succinct, and linked in every way possible, but God has another plan, and it is all good.

> There is a way which seemeth right unto a man,
> but the end thereof are the ways of death.
> (Prov. 14:12)

> It has to look like it is going to work in order for
> it to deceive you. Looks can be deceiving.

31. The way of God may be simple, but it's not easy.

32. Sometimes, certain things or certain people must move before other things came come.

33. Who is it that you are allowing to be your placeholder? Who is blocking the real move of God in your life? The wrong job? Man? Woman? Beliefs?

34. Delays should not be considered as denials by God.

> Keep asking, seeking, and knocking.

35. God does not have multiple-choice options for living life.

For all the promises of God in him are yea, and in him Amen, unto the glory of God by us.
(2 Cor. 1:20)

36. Memory was given to us by God but not so we could relive the past and go into a spiral of depression. Our memory should recount all the goodness of the Lord and how He brought us out with a mighty, outstretched hand. It should remind us of how He has caused us to prosper and how we should love people as He loved us.

37. Get so busy living in the present and looking forward to the future that there is no time for the past.

38. All things work together for you in the Lord... not just the good things!

And we know that all things work together for good to them that love God, to them who are the called according to his purpose. (Rom 8:28)

God is our refuge and strength, a very present help in trouble. Therefore will not we fear, though the earth be removed, and though the mountains be carried into the midst of the sea; Though the waters thereof roar and be troubled, though the mountains shake with the swelling thereof. Selah. There is a river, the streams whereof shall make glad the city of God, the holy place of the tabernacles of the most High. God is in the midst of her; she shall not be moved: God shall help her, and that right early. The heathen raged, the kingdoms were moved: he uttered his voice, the earth melted. The Lord of hosts is with us; the God of Jacob is our refuge. Selah. (Psa. 46:1-7)

For all things are for your sakes, that the abundant grace might through the thanksgiving of many redound to the glory of God.
(2 Cor. 4:15)

Wherefore gird up the loins of your mind, be sober, and hope to the end for the grace that is to be brought unto you at the revelation of Jesus Christ. (1 Pet. 1:13)

39. God never sleeps, nor does He take vacations. I, therefore, encourage you to sleep well and take a break. There's no need for both of you to be awake and work all the time.

FINAL THOUGHT

God is not holding anything against us, so choose to go forward in daily victory. That's a powerful statement. God is not holding anything against you.

So many people have said this storm came because God was holding something against the city. It was wicked and perverse and not obeying Him. This is simply not the truth. If that were the case, every city that is doing things contrary to the will of God would have to face the same judgment and punishment seen in Katrina.

How can I say this was not true?

> But now hath he obtained a more excellent ministry, by how much also he is the mediator of a better covenant, which was established upon better promises. For if that first covenant had been faultless, then should no place have been sought for the second. For finding fault with them, he saith, Behold, the days come, saith the Lord, when I will make a new covenant with the house of Israel and with the house of Judah: Not

according to the covenant that I made with their fathers in the day when I took them by the hand to lead them out of the land of Egypt; because they continued not in my covenant, and I regarded them not, saith the Lord. For this is the covenant that I will make with the house of Israel after those days, saith the Lord; I will put my laws into their mind, and write them in their hearts: and I will be to them a God, and they shall be to me a people: And they shall not teach every man his neighbour, and every man his brother, saying, Know the Lord: for all shall know me, from the least to the greatest. For I will be merciful to their unrighteousness, and their sins and their iniquities will I remember no more. (Heb. 8:6-12)

Once and for all, God sent His Son into the world to answer the sin question. Jesus paid the full price. He paid it all at the cross of Calvary so we would never be required to pay. Because He paid it all, we will not pay again.

We have a new Covenant with better promises. This Covenant promises that, even though we did wrong, God will not hold the offense against us in the past, present, or future. Why? Because that Covenant promise has been made through Jesus' body and blood.

God said that He would be merciful in the face of our unrighteousness. Our sins and iniquities will He remember "no more." In the Greek language, "no more" means "no more." In Texas, where I was raised, it means "no more." And now, here in Louisiana, it means "no more." Therefore, I can safely say that God is not holding anything against you. So, go and live a guilt-free and condemnation-free life in Jesus' name.

Lastly, let me make it clear that I am not encouraging you to go and just do anything you want, live any kind of life you want, or sin whenever you want because God is not holding anything against you. Sin cannot wipe out God's grace and forgiveness, but sin has consequences and will unravel your life if sin is what you choose. In other words, if you choose to murder someone, you are forgiven in God, but you will pay the consequences of being given life in prison, locked up and forgiven.

God will cause us to know of His goodness because He has shown to us such great mercy and amazing grace. This kind of mercy and grace must be responded to in kind.

About the Author

Dr. Lance Alexander is Senior Pastor of Rivers of Life Church International (Shreveport, Louisiana). He has been a passionate Christian leader for over 30 years and now serves his community, pastors, and families by helping them to "transition" through life's struggles.

Lance earned a Bachelor of Science in Industrial Technology from Prairie View A&M University (Texas), a Bachelor of Theology from Heart of America College (Missouri), and a Masters and Doctorate of Philosophy from Heritage International Bible College (Tennessee).

He currently resides in Louisiana with his wife, Vernell M. Alexander. She is his great friend, supporter, and confidant.

www.ingramcontent.com/pod-product-compliance
Lightning Source LLC
LaVergne TN
LVHW091257080426
835510LV00007B/292